The Secret Grotto

Dare to Believe!

William J. Marohnic

Iron Sentinel Publishing – Glasgow, KY
ISBN: 978-0-692-07253-0
Library of Congress Control Number:
2018904338
The Secret Grotto | William Marohnic
Digital distribution | Paperback
Iron Sentinel Publishing, 2017

Dedication

To those faithful stewards that brought discovery and enlightenment to the mystery.

Introduction

In this true and inspiring story the reader will be challenged to "dare to believe." The account centers on a mysterious, yet enchanting secluded cave nestled in south central Kentucky's cave country. A large and beautifully stunning cavern; so pleasing to the eye but strangely sheltered; hidden away from unrestricted view.

Even now, amidst the bustle of Kentucky cave tourism; this vast and ornate cavern has escaped any ravages of commercialism and remains a place where time in fact, does seem to have stood still. No doubt, this has been significant in maintaining the captivating mystery which surrounds this secret cave.

Here begs the question, why has this cavern been spared the indignities and garish realities of cave exploitation and commercialization for profit? Is it plausible that this enigmatic shrouded grotto has since the dawning age of antiquity, been predestined for a higher purpose? Is there to be revealed a Divine design, orchestrated by the hand of providence, which transcends the ages?

In this remarkable story, this once reclusive cavern would for purposes known only to its Creator, begin to divulge its long guarded secrets from within. Through modern day discovery and enlightenment, a slowly emerging legacy would unravel the historic relationship between the grotto and the areas earliest human inhabitants. It was here man and God through nature would bond, traversing the centuries together in a mutually compatible fellowship.

The cave's secrets begin to be shared with the outside world as a faint whisper; much like the gentle breeze which greeted the emerging leaves on the surrounding towering walnut and oak trees; that perfect spring southern Kentucky morning in 1988. This was the day the very first cave survey and mapping began. At the request of and through the efforts of a local hobbyist grotto group, the long unknown and uncharted mysteries found within the cavern, would soon be authenticated. With this process, the cave was officially designated to be a Native American Sacred Site Cave. This rare distinction would change everything.

No one could have predicted or even imagined the magnitude of the exciting chain of events, and the far reaching humanitarian outcomes revealed through the secrets; so long guarded within this cave. I am a witness; God unlocks secrets for the good of humankind. Dare to believe!

Table of Contents
Chapters

Acknowledgements

I would be remiss not to acknowledge the Green River Grotto Survey Team that discovered so much more than was presently known, about this mysterious cave during their mapping survey in 1988. At the time, we had no idea that these discoveries would unleash an astonishing and unexpected sequence of events never imagined.

On a personal note, I must express gratitude to a very special small group of contemporary Native American Shaman Priests who visited the cave site in early 1989. Being a novice cave owner, I lacked perspective of what a sacred site cavern truly encompassed. These well-informed Holy Men spent the better portion of a day endeavoring to enlighten me about their inherited history of the significance of Native American sacred sites. I remain forever grateful to them.

On that day as we lingered within the cave, they marveled at the raw untamed natural beauty and opulence which enveloped us.

Moreover, they were moved and inspired by what they could not see, yet sensed there in the total darkness of the cave. They felt a high spiritual energy; a Holy omnipresence resonating throughout the cavern's cathedral sized rooms and high domed ornate ceilings, as beams from a single flashlight added some illumination to our immediate surroundings. They told me of many sacred site caves they had visited and talked about their purpose as worship sites; a special designated place to acknowledge and pay tribute to God the Creator; not unlike man-made churches of today.

The Shaman Priests believed this cave to be a more exalted and very rare place; a favored Holy site. They believed it to be a place for all important Deity worship and Deity emulation. That is, not just limited to worship and praise Holiness, but to elevate one's self to a higher spiritual purpose in an attempt to live a purposeful life. They concluded this cave was without doubt a Holy sanctuary of the highest order, thus requiring modern day protection and preservation.

Upon their departure, one of the priests shook my hand and said, "Good luck in your new life as the gatekeeper of this Holy Site." All these years later, these words still resonate and echo in my thoughts, as does my remembrance of them leaving the darkness of the cave and emerging into the late afternoon fading light.

Hesitant to leave, I continued to linger in the cave's vestibule appreciating a few moments of solitude in the semi-darkness. I reconsidered the sacred traditions and ceremonies that had been practiced here at this cave site, by untold generations of ancient North American Indian peoples. This encounter with the Shaman Priests would significantly influence my evolving stewardship role for this distinctive sacred site cave; which for a brief earthly measure of time had been placed in my charge.

Suddenly my mood darkened; as I recalled the more recent happenchance of this cave which had been fraught with human exploitation, looting and desecration. I then realized it was my responsibility to put an end to the insult to this Holy site. The recognition was unsettling as I believed I was the least equipped or prepared to rise to this challenge.

To begin, I had no expertise in any field relating to anything about caves. I had no means or connections to mount a rescue and rehabilitation effort. In short, in the world of cave conservation and preservation, I was alone, truly a nobody, not even sure of my own resolve. Yet, the site was far too important to just leave with disregard, vulnerable to further destructions through neglect. I realized what was needed was nothing short of a miracle. This work would require a small army of stewards with know-how and resources in order to stop and reverse the downward spiral. Surely it would take an act of providence to return the sacred site back to God's purpose; a special sanctuary where the Creator God was coveted above all things. In essence, this was His divine earthly house which He surely would not forsake.

Sadly, my moment of faith inspiration waned; soon clouded by human doubt, leaving me with mere wishful thinking. Nevertheless, I was hopeful; and I remembered a quote from Alexander Pope's, **Essay on Man**, "Hope springs eternal in the human breast." In those early days, hope rooted in faith, was to be my sole ally.

September 17, 2017

Chapter I

Nature's Embrace

It was the spring of 1988, and with the purchase of a small farm in South Central Kentucky, happily I started a new chapter in my life.

The long eight year nightmare had finally ended. My career as a Social Worker, which culminated as a whistleblower, had been filled with conflict, drama, and hardship. Mercifully, that chapter had ended. Now ready to pick up the pieces of my life at forty, I longed for a new peaceful, and fruitful, existence for myself and family.

Fate, it seemed, had led me to this farm. My twenty year old son, Nicholas, had told me of a farm property which was to be sold at auction, outside the nearby small town of Smiths Grove. He and a friend, had looked at the farm, and were impressed with the old antebellum house and barns. However, he was most excited about a cave that was located within a wooded area, not too far from the house.

Nicholas and his friend had actually ventured into the front section of the cave, and he excitedly described the large rooms and tall ceilings they viewed with their flashlight. He urged me to check out the property before the day of the auction, which was fast approaching. Initially, I had resisted his suggestion, but as a result of his persistence that I investigate "his find", and a week of hounding me to at least drive by the property, I relented for the most part to placate him.

It was an early April morning that I first ventured to the farm. No one was around, as I drove up the long driveway. The two story white house had a stately appearance, and was framed by several mature trees with an expansive green lawn. The out buildings and barns were painted and well maintained. As I gazed about, my eyes focused on a large forested sink hole, which consisted of about two acres.

A small trail, I viewed just inside the expanse of trees, seemed to be inviting me to follow, and become engulfed by the tranquility offered within. The pathway was flanked with a dazzling montage of brightly colored wildflowers, which were slightly perfuming the morning air. A vast songbird population, chirping and singing their melodies, coaxed me further down the enticing path.

The Nature trail leading to The Secret Grotto

This felt like a type of Eden, and I knew instinctively this was a very special place. It seemed absent of the intrusion of modern man. There existed here, a timeless quality that seemed to pull one into its embrace, bombarding the senses along the way.

I continued down the trail, going deeper into

this natural paradise, when abruptly came upon the entrance to the cave. The cool cave air bellowed from of the cave mouth. Wild hydrangea with tangling long vines draped over the opening. Sunbeams danced through the floral drapery, highlighting hundreds of tiny delicate white flowers, creating a lace-like embellishment on the ground. Miniscule water droplets showered the entry, echoing the sounds from a distant stream within.

The realization amazed me that just a few hundred feet from this natural garden, ran a blacktop road traveled regularly by countless vehicles and people. However, the sensation of standing within a God made sanctuary was overwhelming.

The surrounding trees were magnificent. Most were ancient Oaks, huge in diameter and exceedingly tall, they provided a protective shading of the trail and dense flora. Strong, imposing, and hundreds of years old, it crossed my mind that these trees existed before George Washington's time. Amazed they had survived the logger's chainsaw, I suddenly felt an urge to protect them; knowing that they were not mine to protect.

My grandchildren, many years later, would call these trees, "the grandfather trees". One occasion, I was approached by commercial loggers to buy the timber. Although I could have used the extra money at the time, I was never tempted to see these magnificent trees suffer such a fate. I still carried that protective feeling within my heart.

However, that early April morning, I did not know what the future held. I was intent at that moment to approach the cave mouth; peering inside, the cave faded into darkness. Sunlight invaded the entrance, casting shadows and reaching inside only a hundred feet or so. The sunbeams seemed to stretch as far as they could, only to be stopped abruptly by the overwhelming darkness. The cave darkness reigned here, with its own alien and foreboding world. Instinctively, caution becomes the prowess for the potential invader.

With flashlight in hand, I turned slightly in order to look over my shoulder for one last glimpse of daylight. I delighted in the instant awareness of the majesty of nature; as my senses were overwhelmed with a spectacle of natural beauty; the sweet-smelling scent of blossoms, and the harmonious chorus of singing birds.

I had a new found appreciation for the morning sun, whose filtered rays highlighted a kaleidoscopic view of dazzling flora, which were responsible for the intoxicating fragrance drifting into the darkness where I stood. My eyes focused on a massive stately oak tree; home to a variety of wildlife including squirrels and those delightful song birds who continuously proclaim the joy of life.

Prudently, I made my way into the increasing coolness of this black alien cavern; a bit unnerved and anxious as to what might be encountered ahead. Local folktales circulated in the small rural town nearby, had overtime made the cave locally infamous; as stories were passed around about mysterious vanishings of alleged cave explorers who could not be accounted for. The cave's mystique had become magnified, as one or two of the previous owners forbade any public access; sometimes running the trespassers off the property at the end of a shotgun barrel.

White Oak Tree on Nature Trail 1988

I was not properly equipped to venture any further into the black void. As I retraced my steps up the path back to modern society, I had an urge to linger a bit longer, but forged on feeling the loosing of Nature's embrace. Reaching the top of the sinkhole, I heard a voice.

An elderly lady approached me, shouting, "You are trespassing!" "Get off of my property!"

I could see anger in her facial features, but also a deeper sadness and hurt in her eyes. She was preparing herself for the necessary loss of her farm in the upcoming auction. I felt compassion for her and naturally apologized for the intrusion. Later I learned that the sale of the property was a "forced sale" and that her husband had recently died.

As I left that day, I planned to attend the auction, but did not believe I would be able to afford the property, but secretly dared to hope that there was a chance.

Two weeks later I attended the auction, and what I considered to be nothing short of a miracle, I placed a successful bid, purchasing the house and cave plus seventeen acres of the two hundred sixty acre farm. Some may call it fate, but I believe it was God's hand that brought me to this farm; changing my life forever.

Soon after moving in, Nicholas and I excitedly made our plans to explore the cave. We had little information from which to proceed, but had heard from a few locals that a string of previous owners had attempted to keep the cave closed from curiosity seekers. For our initial exploration, we prepared for an all-day event, packing our supply bags with several light sources, food and water.

Upon entering the cave vestibule, we spotted two very large wooden barrels or tanks. There was a pipe atop one of the tanks which we followed to a small waterfall. The piping was amassing water and funneling it several feet, into the collection barrel. This water assemblage system dated back to the latter part of the nineteenth century. The engineering involved was impressive.

We were amazed at the size of this first room. It was huge, at least thirty feet wide, with a twenty foot high ceiling. The main trunk of the cave, extended for several hundred feet from the entrance. A semi-truck could easily pass the length of this shaft. Making our way further into the cave, we saw a scattering of bones along the walkway.

We began to hear what sounded like the rush of water. As we proceeded, with the sound intensifying, we discovered the source. Turning a corner, we saw it! There a vast fifty foot high waterfall impressed into a cove of the cave wall, was producing a massive amount of water pouring down into a gigantic pool, as the acoustics of the cave amplified the sound of the falling water, creating a thunderous roar.

The Secret Grotto Winter Scene 1989

There were smooth rock carvings everywhere, created by the force of water constructing lasting impressions over the passing centuries. The water was crystal clear and quite cool.

The further we traveled into the cave, the higher the ceiling became. Switching off our lights, we were engulfed in an exaggerated blackness, which I had never before experienced. A sensation of insignificance overwhelmed me, in the presence of the raw power and expansiveness of this environment. Feeling slightly intimidated the urge to press on permeated my instincts, as though being dared by some unidentified life-force to go further.

At this point, we had passed about two thousand feet into the cave. We commented on how fresh the air was, absent of peculiar odors. Life signs appeared in the form of cave crickets clinging to the walls and the passage of an occasional bat flying by.

The path before us started to fill with huge rocks and boulders. The terrain was shifting as we entered a colossal canyon room, which dropped a couple of hundred feet, having a sixty foot ceiling. The width of the walls was at least fifty feet. The center of the ceiling poured forth yet another massive waterfall. It was breathtaking. I had the sense of being in a cathedral room. Sadly, it was obvious this wonderful room had been used by local youth over the years for parties. Trash and beer cans littered the ground. The area had been desecrated and fouled by thoughtless people.

This area of the cave is particularly spectacular. The overwhelming sense of the wonder and power of nature, surely awed early Native American's by the display of such beauty.

Moving on, the terrain began to change once again. We entered a room with deep pits and sudden drop-offs. Caution had to be used with every step. Passing a beam on the walls from our light source, we noticed at the very top of a canyon wedged in a crevice, was a large tire. It was definitely out of place. The only logical explanation had to be that it had rested there at some earlier time when the cave had become flooded. We estimated the height of the water level had reached at least fifty feet, in order for the tire to be lodged on the cliff wall. The volume of water to fill that huge room to that height had to be enormous. Evidence of modern man's trash, in the otherwise beautiful and pristine setting, was symbolic and disturbing. The cave seemed to point out man's destructive and careless nature, showcased for all to see.

We were beginning to see a vast amount of graffiti on the cave walls. There was a marked contrast between the historical and contemporary wall markings. The current graffiti reflected block lettering, crude and simplistic juvenile vulgarisms. The historic markings displayed a more elegant handwriting skill and were void of vulgarity. In fact, many of these writings were Biblical verses or poetical. The presentation is a visual depiction of man's digression to a more vulgar and inarticulate nature, as demonstrated simply by the graffiti style and message.

Some of the earliest writings were dated as being done in the 1820's. It is important to note, that the graffiti is located in one small section, with the vast majority of the cave being untouched with such markings. Taking time for a break, we sat upon a large rock, which resembled a coffin.

Turning off our lights, we became silent. The sensation of complete darkness, once again flooded our senses. We listened to the cave noises. The echoes of the water dripping and flowing were very soothing. The temperature within the cave was a constant fifty-four degrees. There was a slight dampness in the air. I could smell a faint musky odor emanating from the walls and floor.

Although feeling surprisingly peaceful, I had the strong impression of being in an alien world, not natural or conducive to man. There was an ambiance that time, as we count it, did not exist or even mattering this world. Geological time prevailed here. A century of contemporary time is but a tick on the geologic clock, making the life span of a man seem even more insignificant.

Gathering our gear, we proceeded to move forward with our exploration. Approaching a narrowing of the cave trunk, I turned to take in one last look at the massive room we would be leaving, before moving on. I gazed in wonder at the huge circular ceiling resembling a perfectly sculptured dome, polished smooth by a skilled hand. Suddenly, a lone bat appeared, gliding high above, casting its shadow on the dome. The fluttering of wings and its erratic chirping, interrupting the silence when momentarily caught in the beam from the flashlight.

The direction we now took went abruptly to the right. The cave trunk at some point in the past had shifted its course radically, inconsistent with the straight and gradual flow emanating from its inception at the mouth. I was no Geologist, but this seemed very odd to me. I was aware that flowing water was the force cutting through the limestone which resulted in the formation of this cave, over an extensive passage of time. Thus far, we had seen a gradual arching of the walls with no other area yielding to a sharp directional change. This sudden turn to the right, was puzzling and added to the mystique of the cave.

Just as we were moving on, my eye caught one more sensational feature. At the top of the canyon rock wall, at least sixty feet up from the floor was a depiction of a cross. The lines of this formation were almost perfectly straight; both vertically and horizontally. As we focused both of our flashlight beams on this area, we could clearly see this was a deep carving into the rock. It essentially was two naturally formed shafts, one horizontal and one vertical, both perfect in length and width producing the Christian icon. So perfect, it appeared to have been intentionally inscribed, but due to its location, it had to be a natural formation, created solely by water dissolving the limestone over the passage of thousands of years.

Wanting to linger and marvel at this wonderful mystery, I was reminded we had to move on. Our rations and lighting capability was limited and we soon would need to turn back. As we traversed the cave path, we soon had to stoop down and practically crawl through an increasingly tight space. This tapered way continued for several hundred feet, and I began to suspect this gradual narrowing may be signaling the end of the cave. Just as abruptly as the way had constricted, it opened into another large room with the sounds of flowing, cascading water.

Moving forward, Nicholas and I noticed the cave floor becoming sandy, transforming into a beach-like surface. Scanning the darkness with our flashlights, to our amazement we were looking at a small lake or pond. The light reflecting onto the darkness opened for us a picture of clear water which had a beautiful aqua tint graduating to a deep blue at the center of the lake. In the middle of this lake was a very small island, which appeared to be about ten feet in diameter. To our amazement, in the water we saw several, pure white medium sized fish, some about twelve inches long and they appeared to weigh three to five pounds. The fish had no eyes. I wondered what they ate; how they were sustained. They appeared perfectly healthy, swimming about in the water, with no need for sight as their existence was in absolute darkness. They possessed another means of maneuvering about, avoiding collision and recognizing a food source using a sense other than vision. Indeed, another wonder of this splendid underground world!

As the beams from our flashlights pierced the darkness, in a corner of the room we spotted a huge crystal like formation overhanging the lake. This formation had a resemblance of the head of an elephant with its trunk falling downward toward the water. I recalled a cave guide saying it took about a hundred years to grow one inch of cave formations. This particular creation had to be fifty feet in total length; therefore, it must have taken thousands of years to develop into this present form.

The Lake Room
Photo Courtesy of: Dr. Chris Groves – 1989

The splendor of this lake, coupled with the magnificent overhanging formation, left us breathless. I was flooded with joy, at the realization that this cave was now a part of my life. I also felt a growing sense of responsibility, knowing I would need to become a steward of this natural wonder. The idea that I actually owned the cave, escaped me. It is too big and significant to be thought of in that way. One can only serve as a temporary overseer for a brief period of time, in context to the ageless life of this cave. With these thoughts swirling about in my mind, we sat down on the sandy shore of the lake, again turning off our flashlights.

The darkness was all encompassing. The water sounds were soothing, encouraging the overwhelming feeling of contentment. These sounds, if captured on tape, would make the perfect bedside sleeping aide. Momentarily, I thought I heard the muffled sound of voices. Nicholas thought he heard the same thing. This could only be attributed to our overactive imaginations in this mood altering scenery. These unique sounds were likely created as a result of the gentle wind currents bouncing off the cave walls.

The embrace of our surroundings seemed to cast an intoxicating spell over us, cleansing our senses. Wishing to linger indefinitely in this tranquility, we needed to move on. To maneuver around the lake, we had to climb up a narrow path and round the water by carefully side stepping on a six inch wide pathway, while clinging to the cave wall in order to prevent slipping into the lake. It was a little daunting, but we managed the passage without incident.

This outer room, as we moved past the lake became rocky with deep pits on either side. Although the cave passage appeared to continue indeterminately, we stopped to access our situation. We made the decision to turn back, realizing we were ill equipped to go further.

Retracing our steps, we were giddy with the excitement of all we had seen.

We began to quicken our pace, but noticed we had a different view of the cave features as we traveled in this reverse direction. The sheer enormity of the cave rooms seemed even more evident. Everything about this cave was big and dramatic. This cave could easily be called, "the cave with big shoulders". The ceilings and walls were sculptured, as if shaped by an artist completing a masterpiece. Each colossal room with the high domed ceiling, created a sense of being in a great cathedral. For the most part, the cave passages had been relatively wide, level, and easy to traverse. The air within was clean, free of any polluting odors. The waterfalls were breathtaking, boasting thunderous clear and sparkling water flows. The artificial light from a flashlight, fashioned a subtle glow that danced off the walls and ceiling.

However, as accommodating as the cave had been to our intrusion, it would not give up its hidden treasures easily. Overpowering darkness is its main defense, ever present, hinting that constant danger looms, so one is prudent to proceed with caution and reverence.

A small waterfall streaming from a 60 foot cave wall

As we approached the cave vestibule, natural light form the sun flooded the entrance. Reflecting on the day's events, I was glad to have shared this experience with my son, knowing we would remember our day of exploration the rest of outlives.

At that particular time of my life, I had not given God His rightful place in leading me; however, the day spent in the cave, amidst all the natural beauty, left me feeling I had been in the presence of a superior force, far beyond man's authority.

Beyond the black and white scientific geological justifications of how the cave came into existence, what resonated with me was the indescribable beauty I had witnessed, which defied logical explanation.

Hiking up the trail, choking with its dense flora, it was fascinating to realize how this vast cave was hidden so precisely within the natural surface terrain. The house and highway were but a short distance from the cave mouth, but the contrast between these two worlds was vivid.

Sunset approached as we neared the house. We were both tired and hungry, but already I was eagerly anticipating my next journey into the cave.

The following week I kept a hectic schedule settling into our new home. As busy as I was with everyday activities, my thoughts often wandered back to that first day of exploration in the cave. It almost seemed as if it had been a dream, and I had been suddenly awakened to the mundane reality of twentieth century life.

One night I was awakened to the agitated barking of my dogs. Reluctantly leaving the comfort of my bed, I went outside to investigate the ruckus. The dogs were excited to the level of a fevered pitch. They were contained within a fenced area, but their attention was directed toward the cave area of the property. It was almost two o'clock in the morning, with an early spring chill in the night air. The moon was full, so the dogs were visible in the moonlight.

I went back inside the house to retrieve a jacket and a flashlight, in order to attempt to identify the basis of all this commotion. Cautiously navigating the trail down toward the cave, the milieu of the night was in stark contrast to the more inviting sensations felt in the warmth of the sunlight during the day. As I approached the cave mouth, all appeared undisturbed and quiet. Everything seemed to be sleeping within the forest, with only a couple of rabbits scooting across the path, as the flashlight provided me a glimpse of the white of their tails.

As I began my retreat back toward the house, I heard voices coming from the direction of the road above where I stood, along with the sound of a car trunk or door slamming shut. I rushed back to the house and jumped into my truck, driving the length of the long driveway to the country road adjoining the front of the farm. Turning onto the road, the lights of an unfamiliar vehicle flashed toward me, as it abruptly pulled out from the corner of my property. The car sped by me, accelerating and burning rubber from the tires, determined to escape identification.

As the car zipped past, for a split second I could make out the silhouettes of four individual's heads. I made a quick turnaround in my truck, intent on following the car, but was not fast enough, only seeing their taillights disappear into the darkness of the night.

I knew they were trespassers, invading the cave and up to no good. Their activity interrupted by the incessant barking of the dogs, and they likely heard me coming down the trail as I proceeded with my investigation. Anger welled up in me. I was outraged that these strangers were invading my sanctum. There was a feeling of personal violation, and I wanted to strike back and protect what was mine.

As I drove back to the house, I grasped this new disturbing and unanticipated problem. How was I to confront this? The cave and all its possessions seemed to be vulnerable to thieves of the night, and I felt helpless.

Daylight confirmed my fears. When I returned to the cave entrance, I found empty beer cans and freshly discarded cigarette butts, carelessly left scattered in the previously unspoiled area. During the next few weeks the problem persisted, with dogs barking, cars appearing and disappearing in the middle of the night, and trash deposits in the cave.

I filed a complaint with the police, to no avail. I strategically placed motion detectors with sirens, hoping to scare the intruders away. They afforded little deterrent. I considered letting the dogs run lose at night, but was fearful they might be poisoned. I posted "No Trespassing" warning signs, which they stole.

With the reoccurring issue of trespassing almost nightly, I was becoming obsessed with putting a stop to it. My days were becoming consumed with ways and means to attack the problem. At the same time, I was in the process of building a small livestock operation. I knew I had to devote more of my time and resources to the farm.

However, the cave and its vulnerability to intruders continued to haunt me. When I bought the property, my main priority was to generate an income from the farm. The cave was more like my personal hobby, until some three months later.

In the latter part of July, I was approached by a commercial cave developer, inquiring if I would consider opening the cave to the public for tours. Being centrally located in Kentucky cave country, only seven miles from Mammoth Cave National Park, he voiced his confidence that the prospect of developing the cave as a business enterprise could be profitable.

Some investment funding would be needed for lighting and trails within the cave, insurance, etc. He assured me that a steady income could be recognized with low overhead expenses. He knew of a couple of prospective investors that might be interested in joining the venture as silent partners. Although initially skeptical, the more I considered the potential of a second source of income from the property, the more enticed I became.

Nicholas and I could be cave tour guides, taking tourists about a thousand feet inside the cave. The beautiful nature trail leading down to the entrance was an added feature. I became more and more captivated with the idea, and I told the developer I would give it serious thought and provide an answer within the next few days.

I had the idea that a steady income from cave tours could support some kind of professional security system which would solve the trespassing dilemma. Two days later, a group of people approached me as I was feeding the cattle.

Chapter II

Into the Unknown

The group introduced themselves as members of a cave grotto club associated with Western Kentucky University. They knew the cave as "Crump's Cave." In the past they had been unsuccessful in their numerous attempts to obtain permission from the previous owners to explore the cave. According to their story, one owner had ordered them from the property with a shotgun!

Knowing of the recent change in ownership, they wanted to introduce themselves and explore the possibility of the new owner being more conducive to allowing the group access to the cave. I was not inclined to allow them cave privileges for a recreational tour. However, the group leader indicated their desire to conduct an extensive survey of the cave, which would be sanctioned by the Geology Department of the University. To their knowledge the cave had never been surveyed, thus very little was known about the cave's geological and archaeological features. They proposed a survey group which would consist of about twenty individuals, and would take approximately thirty days to complete. Additionally, they pledged to clean out any trash or litter found within the cave, as the survey progressed. They possessed notable credentials, including membership and accreditation in several national cave conservation organizations.

Green River Grotto Survey Team 1989

I liked their proposal and their obvious priority for cave preservation and conservation. I had already realized I could use all the help I could get with managing this ever consuming project.

As we discussed the details involved in conducting the survey, I told them about my predicament with the frequency of trespassers invading the cave. Sharing my concern, they offered to assist in any way possible and would monitor the cave as the survey progressed. We set a date of the following Saturday for the survey to commence.

As they left, I felt completely comfortable with my decision authorizing the survey. I was excited with anticipation as to what their work may uncover. I truly believed the exploration and survey would prove to be beneficial for the cave.

Having pondered the prospect of commercial development of the cave, I contacted the fellow who came to me a few days earlier, and requested to meet with the silent partners he had referenced. I wanted an idea of who I would be dealing with. We agreed to meet the following evening at my house.

Sitting around the dining room table, I asked for the particulars, as they perceived them, for a possible commercial cave operation. They both expressed a need to build concrete walkways; install high intensity lighting, and widen the nature trail pathways leading to the cave entrance. They proposed locating a large blacktop parking area at the front of the farm.

In their assessment, the terrain neighboring the cave was too rugged, needing commercial improvement in order to be made suitable for public use. It became clear to me that the set-up costs would be considerable, and their investment marginal.

I had seen other commercial cave operations in the area, set up with the concrete trails poured into the caves making public access less cumbersome and safer. But there was a tradeoff. The more accommodating the modern improvements, the less natural the caves seemed to be, creating a staged atmosphere, replacing the natural setting established with the passage of thousands of years. Man- made alterations would destroy the natural design of Mother Nature. Once these so-called improvements were done, they could not be undone. The natural setting would be lost.

Recalling my very first encounter with the nature trails that wonderful spring morning as I ventured down to the cave mouth, the thought of ripping out much of that natural flora, simply was not acceptable to me. Natural pathways, created by the traipsing of buffalo herds of past times, and maintained by a substantial deer population, were scattered throughout the vast wilderness of Kentucky, linking meadow lands with the forest. I was content with the existing nature trails within my little area of forestry, which were easily cleared of any excessive vegetative overgrowth by a passing with my weed eater.

Thanking them for their ideas and suggestions, I bid them good-by, knowing I likely would not be consulting with them again. If I was to seriously consider offering public cave tours, it would have to be accomplished in a way which would minimize any intrusion to the land. Any notion of a major bustling commercial cave operation just was not going to happen at the expense of disturbing the special features of Nature's artistry and the consequent feeling of serenity which emanated from this place. However, I was still very serious about establishing some kind of commercial cave tour set-up. But I still had my small livestock business to oversee and the cave grotto survey would commence within a few days.

On the morning of the survey, the spelunker team unloaded equipment from two trucks, as the sun arose ushering in a bright warm day. I eagerly greeted them, noting how young they were, as they strapped on their gear. They appeared to be amply prepared with all forms of lighting hardware, hardhats, cameras of various types, and sophisticated looking survey instruments. Each team member was securing on their backs, fully loaded hiking packs, which I presumed contained food, water, and extra clothing. They looked as if they could be setting out for an expedition which would last for days. The team leader, true to his word, distributed to each member several large black trash collection bags. My excitement equaled theirs as preparations were being made to begin the exploration.

I was provided a written list of the functions they would perform as a part of the survey work. The team consisted of geologists, archaeologists, and hydrologists. One member had the sole responsibility to collect air and water samples, which would be used to gauge the level of pollution within the cave. Any trace of chemicals leaching into the cave from surrounding agricultural and farming activities would be analyzed.

A major objective of the survey was to measure the length of the cave, widths of the trunk passages, and ceiling heights. Early local rumors suggested the cave may be several miles long and connect with Mammoth Cave, which was located just a few miles down the road. An additional objective was to inventory the cave for artifacts.

This region of the state is dotted with caves and sinkholes. Native American habitation is well documented; many were cave dwellers often using the caves for shelter and ceremonial activities. Many caves had found to be used as burial sites. In fact, I had recently been cleaning out one of the outbuildings near the house and found within a cardboard box containing several bones which appeared to be human. An expert from the university determined the bones to be the remains of two young females, under twenty years of age at the time of death, which were now several hundred years old. The bones had likely been buried in the cave and had been so well preserved due to the constant temperature and humidity level. They were probably disturbed as a result of cave flooding or human looting. Returning the bones to the cave, we buried them in a remote section.

The survey team comprised of four men and three women slowly entered the cave vestibule and began to methodically take measurements. Their bright lights flooded the room, startling a few cave crickets whose long antenna flickered up and about, as the security of their naturally dark environment was invaded.

Leaving these professionals to their work, I began thinking once again about my trespassing problem, concerned that the interlopers' may disturb the survey markers as well as other equipment left in the cave by the team. I was not the first steward of this cave who was faced with the quandary of trying to control unwanted intrusions onto the property. The Crump family that lived here many years ago must have shared my feelings of frustration and helplessness. Some local old timers' remembered the Crump's constructing a large wooden gate across the cave entrance. Some forty feet in length, and eight feet in height, it was said to be a solid wood barrier with a small locked entry door. Some seventy years later, there were still bits and pieces of decaying wood from the barrier, which remained scattered along the cave entrance.

This action, taken by the Crump family, with the best of intensions to afford some degree of protection for the cave, eventually had a sad ending. The bat population residing within the cave came out nightly to feed, returning at dawn to roost. The solid wood security gate prevented the bats from making their nightly feeding excursions, so ultimately the population died out. Back in that era, sensitivity to bat habitations was not deemed to be of much importance. This is but one example, of a two hundred year testimonial to the rape and pillage done to this cave at the hands of white men. The earlier history of Native Americans, for the most part, indicated the caves were revered as a part of Mother Earth and were considered to be sacred sites.

In today's culture, caves are often vandalized, looted, exploited and polluted. This had become an escalating concern for me since moving to the farm. It seemed fate had assigned me this responsibility and how to effectively deal with the challenge was becoming an ever consuming part of my life. The status quo was unacceptable.

The intruder problem reared its ugly head that very night. It was after midnight the commotion began. The dogs were barking and howling, trying to break free from the pen. Everyone in the house was awakened. All hell seemed to be breaking loose and I had reached the end of my rope! I dressed quickly and impulsively grabbed a rifle, hurriedly making my way down the trail toward the cave. As I reached the cave, the dogs stopped barking and calm settled in. I could see no one, nor hear any voices. Scanning the area with my flashlight while keeping my weapon close, sanity and reason returned as it crossed my mind how vulnerable I was to possible ambush from several men cloaked in the darkness of night. I needed to walk toward the road and see if their car was still there. The trespassers' always park their vehicles in the most secluded and hidden location at the end of the property line.

Climbing up the trail, my heart was racing and my breathing labored as I reached the road. The car was still there, visible by the moonlit night. Using the beam from my flashlight to read the license plate, I realized the car was registered in an adjoining county. The intruders were probably deep into the cave by now. I needed to do something, but knew it would be far too dangerous to venture into the cave alone. The caver's first rule of thumb, is never go caving by yourself.

I decided it was time to involve law enforcement officials. Returning to the house, I made a call to the State Police post, reporting the trespassing on my property. The dispatcher assured me a unit would respond within thirty minutes.

Shortly a cruiser pulled up to the driveway and I met two Troopers on the front porch. It was almost two o'clock in the morning as I began my explanation of the situation, telling the officials the trespassers were in the cave and their car parked boldly on the side road. They too, were reluctant to follow them into the cave and the Troopers 'discussed their options. They wanted me to show them where the car was parked, so I climbed into the back seat of the cruiser and directed them to the vehicle. They inspected the car with their huge flashlights, zooming in at the left rear tire, which was off the road, except for approximately two inches. Talking with each other, they got on their radio, making a call for a tow truck.

They explained that the car was partially parked on the road, which created a potential danger to other moving vehicles, thus justifying the action they had taken in securing the tow truck. I thought this was great! Finally there was some justice and consequence for those criminals!

The Troopers' told me the car would be impounded at the Chevron station a couple of miles up the road, where it would remain confiscated until the owner requested the release in person. I imagined how the intruders' would react when they were ready to leave, finding their car gone. The thought amused me and I could not help but chuckle. My momentary feelings of glee were fleeting, as I realized the cave was still vulnerable to their intrusion and looting.

The survey team had been on site for a few weeks and was making considerable progress. Having completed about a thousand feet inside the cave, they were impressed with the initial findings. The vestibule area revealed several fire hearths uncovered just below the topsoil. This had been a large cooking area for the Native Americans. There, the team had discovered an extensive inventory of cooking utensil artifacts, arrowheads, stone scrapers used for cleaning animal hides, and a various assortment of discarded animal bones and mussel shells brought in from local creeks and rivers. One corner of the room comprised of large mounds of dirt was identified to be composted trash deposits left during the time they inhabited the cave. This area had a small waterfall indented within a cove with a collection pool which provided a convenient water source year round. The nineteenth century pioneer settlers had also taken advantage of this pristine water supply.

Based upon analysis of the animal bones deposited about the fire hearths, deer, rabbit, and squirrel were a food staple for the Native Americans. Sadly, there was considerable evidence of artifact looting within the vestibule room. Team members uncovered at least two pits that had been dugout by hand, to a depth of three feet. These shafts had been made searching for artifacts. Illegal artifact looting in caves is widespread in south-central Kentucky. There has been, and continues to be, an extensive black market for cave artifacts. Most of the best Indian artifacts are found in deep caves. These gems are spared the corrosive damage that afflicts topside artifacts which are exposed to the elements of weather and contact with farm implements. They uncovered a near perfect grinding pestle which was used hundreds of years ago to grind corn. The flat side of the device was worn completely smooth as a result of the grinding motion as the pestle made contact with the side of a bowl stone bowl. Kentucky law makes allowance for all materials recovered by approved scientists to be removed from a cave in order to be cleaned, catalogued, and for era identification. The law stipulates a requirement that any materials removed from a cave, must be returned to the cave within one year.

Unauthorized removals of any cave materials are a violation of law, and subject to prosecution. In the cave country area, some locals have established roadside souvenir stands which display Native American artifacts for sale. They always assert the artifacts were found in a search of plowed farmland. This claim may be true in some instances, but no doubt the unspoiled, well preserved specimens have been illegally obtained by cave looters. The massive plow blades usually deface an artifact of size which rested under topside soil.

The water samples tested contained trace deposits of nitrates and bacteria, consistent with seepage through the limestone rock from the surface farming and livestock practices. The concentration of pollutants, although minimal were sufficient to discourage drinking of the water, even though it was completely clear to the eye and odorless. In essence, the water had been filtered by at least ninety feet of limestone rock, which had partially decontaminated it before reaching the cave waterfall.

An advance party of the survey team had discovered two large bat colonies about three quarters of a mile into the cave. One colony had located in a lower section of the cave and consisted of several hundred bats roosting on the sixty foot high ceiling. Large deposits of bat guano or droppings were in this area of the cave, mounded into high foul- smelling piles.

The second colony was detected in a side

room which was somewhat smaller. A member of the grotto group was a biology graduate student at Western Kentucky University. He identified two distinct bat species; a large colony of gray bats, and a smaller Indiana bat colony. Both species were federally protected on the endangered species list. This was considered to be a major find, and the team was very excited about the discovery.

Apparently, the bats were seasonal residents, arriving at the cave during March, establishing maternity colonies. During summer months the bats raised their young, known as "pups." The mother's carried the pups on their backs, flying about taking the infants along for the ride. They would leave the cave each night to feed on various insects, with a particular appetite for mosquitoes. It has been estimated that a single bat can consume their body weight in insects, during the course of a night's feeding.

A State biologist was called in the following week, confirming the species identification made by the graduate student. A precise measurement of the guano mounds was taken which was used to arrive at a population count of near one thousand bats. There is a smaller population of brown bats in the cave, which are not considered to be endangered, and appear to be thriving.

The bats would leave the cave in early November, to return the following March and repeat the cycle of increasing their populace. The frequent human activity of trespassers concerned the survey group. The bat habitats were established well into the depth of the cave, and in remote areas, which hopefully would provide them sanction from the intrusion of human invaders. Disturbances in the roosting areas could startle the bats, causing the mother's to panic and drop the pups to their death. If environmental instabilities should occur with frequency, the bats would likely abandon the cave.

The survey group took elaborate precautions not to disturb the bat colonies, using red lenses on their lighting gear and being sensitive to keeping noises to a minimum.

The State biologist explained that the bats depart the cave every evening around dusk, traveling from the roost areas deep within the cave, flying through tight cave passages, heading for the cave mouth out into the evening twilight. I was intrigued by this evening ritual and decided to witness it first-hand.

A few days later, Nicholas and I ventured down to the cave just before nightfall. It had rained that afternoon, leaving the ground and foliage damp. The air had been refreshed and the forest night life of crickets, birds, and a scattering of frogs, created a symphony for our enjoyment, as the mammoth great oaks silently cast their shadows.

As we quietly sat on a log near the entrance to the ancient stone faced cave, we heard a faint fluttering of wings and high pitched chirping. Suddenly, a few bats flew out of the cave mouth into the evening twilight, turned about abruptly, returning back into the cave opening.

We quietly moved in closer to the entrance, peering into the cave vestibule with our red lens flashlights. The sight was astounding. Hundreds of bats were gliding about in circular formations, wings fluttering and emitting their chirping sounds which were amplified by the cave's acoustics. The bats suddenly, with a synchronized effort, flew out of the cave in small clusters, disappearing into the descending darkness of night. I could feel them passing by me, so very close, but never making contact. Their incessant squeaking sounds filled my ears. It was a fascinating display of Nature, leaving me to wonder where their travels would take them during the night.

Bats provide an essential link in the chain of

life. Not only do they assist in controlling the insect population, they are second only to bees as pollinators. I had noticed that first summer on the farm; we had very few mosquitoes to contend with during outdoor recreational activities. This was attributable to the bat population in the cave. I wanted these colonies to thrive, and be spared unnecessary intrusions of man, in order to insure their return to the cave year after year.

The survey work proceeded for several more weeks, and they had reached the point of being about one third of the way to completion. They were removing any trash or litter from the cave they came across each day, just as promised. I was impressed with their findings thus far, and their commitment to cleaning up the cave interior.

About a week later, I received a telephone call one night from the survey team leader. He told me he had run across an archaeological article in a professional journal, which grabbed his interest. The article, published in the 1970's, was written by a well-known archeologist teaching at a university in Missouri. The author described several specific locations in southeastern states; the university was looking at to commence research in the fall of 1973. They had visited my cave and obtained permission to investigate the site in order to determine its suitability for the project. They had been impressed with the cave vestibule, deciding the cave would be acceptable as an archaeological research venture. The university planned to return in three months to begin their projected seven day on-site survey.

According to the author, upon their return in the fall, they were shocked by what they found. Much of the vestibule room was disturbed and trashed. They found three deep pits had been dug which were about six feet deep, with a three foot circumference. Shovels had apparently been used to gouge out layers of soil, in order to recklessly sift for artifacts. They learned that the farm tenants had vacated the property for approximately two months, leaving the cave vulnerable to looting and destruction.

There had been activity at the very front left wall section of the vestibule. The ground soil in this one hundred square foot area was soft and had obviously been dug out and turned. The archeologist author, speculated this may have been a burial site, but there was no evidence of bones being found at the time of the fall inspection. As a result of this demolition and likely pilferage, the research project scheduled in the cave was scratched. This is the same area; the current survey group believed may have been used by Native Americans as a garbage depot which had composted with the passage of many hundreds of years.

I had heard stories from local folk, that the cave had several burial locations near the front entrance. A group of old timers congregated at a local hardware store. I had often seen them sitting around an old potbellied stove in the store, talking and drinking coffee. I decided to go to the store and hopefully catch them one morning. They may be able to share with me, rumors they had heard about the cave. Everyone in our small town knew of the cave, and its local history.

Later in the week, I needed to purchase some bales of hay at the hardware store, so I scheduled my arrival for early morning, in hopes of encountering this group. Upon arriving, I noticed three of the men sitting together, drinking their morning coffee. After a friendly greeting, I brought up the subject of the cave, which obviously perked their interest, and started a lively discussion of their cave explorations and ventures. They voiced a yearning to be able to explore the cave once more, but had resigned themselves long ago, to the reality that they were now too old for such exploits, and could only reminisce about their past adventures. Their memories were sharp and they were able to recall many details of the things they had seen during many visits to the cave. These men were lifelong residents of the county and knew about all the caves in the area.

They swore my cave was the most beautiful! Some of the area's caves were bigger, some smaller. Some had more spectacular formations, but Crump's cave was the most special due to the cathedral sized rooms which seemed to have been sculptured. They recalled the lake room, with its deep blue water and the single vast crystal- like formation which hung above the lake.

I asked if they had ever seen evidence of any burial grounds within the cave. One of the men, named Henry, clearly recalled an incident he would never forget which he said "left a bad taste in my mouth even to this day."

He began explaining that about forty years ago, he was approaching the cave early one morning for an expedition. As he reached the cave entrance, he observed several men huddled, talking and smoking cigarettes near the entry. Henry greeted them with "Howdy". They seemed startled initially, but responded cordially. Boldly without hesitation, they shared with Henry the treasures they were uncovering from their digging in the cave. They said they had been digging this area all night, taking a break only because they had become tired and hungry. Showing no concern or remorse about their activity, they were quite proud of the bounty they had accumulated.

Near where they stood, was a canvas tarp, according to Henry's recollections. The man standing closest to the tarp abruptly grasped the corner of the material, flipping it back, exposing the night's collection. Henry was surprised to see several human skulls lined up in a neat row. Seeing the expression on his face, the men began to laugh, claiming there was a great demand for real human skulls, which could be converted to use as coffee table ashtrays! I wondered what kind of people would perpetuate such a market demand, and what kind would see to it the need was met? The old timer's in the store, upon hearing this, shook their heads in a semblance of some disgust. They had grown up in another era, but instinctively knew this was wrong. Henry left the cave that morning, never to forget the morbid occurrence he had just witnessed, and the insensitive display of humor and the greed espoused by the looters.

I had to conceal the disgust and indignation I

was feeling. Like Henry, I too was left with a very bad taste in my mouth. I wondered if the men who had worked all night so diligently to uncover these human skulls they would sell to be used as ashtrays for someone's coffee table, would have been so gleeful if the skulls had been looted by others from their family's cemetery. Driving back to the farm, I realized I had left my bales of straw at the store. Somehow, it did not matter right now.

Arriving home, I immediately walked down to the cave. Arriving at the mouth, I saw several sparrows dipping their beaks into tiny pools of water that had been collected beneath the cascading water droplets running down the face of the cave. The scene was so peaceful. I pondered, over time how much pillage and raping had taken place at this very spot, at the hand of man? As I stared, the front of the cave seemed to become transformed into the weather worn face of an old, old man; tears running down his cheeks to be taken up by the birds. This old man's face had also been witness to Henry's early morning encounter some forty years ago.

Walking up the nature trail, to return to the house, I felt ashamed that I had held inside me, the outrage I felt at the store. I made an oath, to be a better steward of the cave, and to take this responsibility more seriously. To the Native Americans this had been a sacred site, which had become desecrated with the incursion of the white man.

I was consumed with thoughts related to this unnerving information I had learned that morning. It was distracting me from properly attending to the real life demands of the day, as if two opposing forces were tugging at me.

The next day, I shared the story Henry had told me with the survey team. Early on in the survey, they had sifted through the soil at the identified site, finding no intact human bones. However, bits and fragments of suspected bone slivers were found. They concurred that this very well could have, in fact been a burial site rather than a composted garbage depository.

Chapter III

Finding God in the Dark

The following day, the survey group planned to commence work in a new location of the cave. The area was beyond the lake room and they had measured the distance to be a little over a mile from their present site. This section was very remote and difficult to reach, as the wide trunk pathway leaving the vestibule had been eventually replaced with exceedingly narrow, less stable undefined paths. The team was eager to explore this unchartered location.

They had prepared and equipped for a hard day of survey work. Extra lighting and food, along with a double supply of water had been crammed into their backpacks.

Much later in the day as I was mowing the lawn, one of the survey team appeared and commenced waving his arms to get my attention. He rapidly made his way to where I had stopped the mower, somewhat out of breath and excited. He said he had come back to the surface to secure a brighter light source. Obviously in a hurry to get back to the cave, he turned around just long enough to shout out that he would be back and give me an update later in the day. They had discovered a low ceiling room, about three hundred feet long, which had sloping walls on each side of its narrow walkway. He said they believed they may be seeing what might be a form of primitive Indian art work. Inhurrt, turned around just long enough to shout out that he would be back and give me an update later in the day.

Indian Mud Glyph Room Entrance (Leaving Lake Room to Glyph Room) Photo courtesy of Karl Niles

As he disappeared from view, I speculated about just how many secrets this cave is guarding. Some think of caves as being merely big holes in the ground. This thinking is flawed. Caves have a story to tell, as each passage harbors abiding riddles and mysteries. I contemplated the significance of unveiling the secrets of this ancient time capsule. The work the grotto team was doing will document and substantiate important archaeological and geological findings, which could herald measures to protect these habitations.

Already the survey has identified endangered bat colonies, which will undoubtedly lead to protective actions. Simple recreational exploration affords no benefit to the cave, thus in my thinking serves no purpose, and can it fact even be distractive. I anxiously awaited word from the team about this new discovery.

That evening they appeared at my door with mud streaked, smiling faces just bursting with excitement. They had found, what they believed was Indian mud glyph art work, spanning a three hundred foot long room, with five foot high slopping walls covered in a green patina. The depictions were obviously very old, and could be rare ceremonial drawings. The authenticity of their speculations would require expert confirmation. They intended to engage the expertise of the Archaeology Department at Western Kentucky University, who would then contact me to arrange a meeting.

The very next morning, I received a call from Valerie Haskins, an archaeology professor with the university. She had expertise in cave archaeology and this was her first semester teaching at Western. She was in her element, being associated with the cave region karst specialists. Having been briefed by the survey group's leader, she explained that if the inscriptions were actually Indian mud glyph drawings, this would be a major discovery. These forms of cave artwork were extremely rare, and very few caves located in the entire southeastern United States, were known to have this type of glyph.

Valerie had already made plans with the survey group to visit the cave and make an assessment of the drawings. If after viewing them, she determined they might be authentic, she would secure the services of an expert in the field to validate the finding.

Later in the week, Valerie and the team made their way back into the cave, staying well into the night. The next day she called, informing me that she believed the drawings were in fact authentic, extremely old; and she would proceed with making the necessary arrangements through the university, to bring in an expert in cave glyphs to officially authentic the find.

The following week, Valerie arrived at the cave in the company of Dr. William Faulkner, a professor with the University of Tennessee, who had the reputation of being the most prominent and highly respected authority on Indian mud glyphs in the entire country. As they entered the cave, I was thinking all these recent happenings seemed to be caught up as a sudden vortex of events, which were proceeding with an accelerated rate of speed. I hoped I was doing the right thing, unleashing these activities involving so many people. However, I must admit I was quite excited with the anticipation of what Dr. Faulkner's opinion would be.

Several hours later, Valerie called me saying they were in route to the airport in Nashville with Dr. Faulkner, who had a scheduled flight returning him home to Knoxville. She said Dr. Faulkner had confirmed, with no question, that the glyphs were indeed authentic, and at least a thousand years old. A more exact age could be established through radio-carbon testing. I felt goose bumps, realizing the significance of this information, but was unaware at the time, just how momentous this would become for the well fare of the cave's future. She asked if I would be agreeable to her involving another cave archaeologist, with a special interest in this area, which was affiliated with the University of Kentucky. Although I wanted to limit the number of people with access to the cave, I agreed to this addition to the emerging research team.

Late each evening, I enjoyed walking down the nature trail to sit by the mouth of the cave to relax and contemplate the events of the day. No question today was a big day. The cave had relinquished yet another hidden secret. I considered the impact of the survey. If no investigation had been conducted, we would never know of these mud glyphs. I felt the increasing responsibility of stewardship for the cave, which resulted from the discoveries which had been made thus far. Consequently, the ever present threat of vandalizing trespassers, weighed heavily on my mind.

During the next two months, word of the discovery of Indian mud glyphs at the cave, had made the rounds with professionals in the fields of archaeology and geology. I had been contacted by representatives from several universities, proposing on-site field studies at the cave. Thanking them for their interest, I declined their offers, intent on maintaining a limit to the number of individuals coming and going at the cave. I decided to limit all field work to be directed through Western Kentucky University. Staff from the geology and archaeology departments would coordinate the cave study.

Valerie and Dan Davis, from the Department of Archaeology at the University of Kentucky, would specifically research the Indian mud glyphs.

It had been the Green River Grotto group who initiated the survey, and are credited with the discovery of the protected bat colonies as well as the Indian mud glyphs. It was their dedication and hard work which ultimately uncovered these cave enigmas.

The scientific cave researchers' were taking a lot of time, logging and reproducing the glyph drawings. They described the glyph area as being a three hundred foot long gallery room. The mud glyphs derive their name from the mud layers on the cave walls, which provided the soft medium for the Indians to make the drawings. The wall mud has a semi-moist texture which acquires a green patina over the span of hundreds of years. These green, textured wall coverings are natural and most prolific in this section of the cave.

Several dozen depictions had been drawn on both walls, traversing the entire length of the gallery. As you walk into the room, the sides of the walls slope outward and upward to the ceiling, from the relatively narrow pathway, creating the appearance of a massive story board of art works to the right and left. The drawings consist of geometric symbols illustrating human figures, warfare scenes, boats, and a variety of animals. According to the experts, the choice of subjects depicted, are most likely ceremonial in nature.

The general consensus of the researchers is that this array of drawings is more detailed and expansive than other regional cave displays. One cave located in Tennessee had been found to contain similar ceremonial drawings, considered to be so rare, that the shaft entrance to the cave was completely sealed closed with cement shutting of the cave from any further entry by man or animal.

Most of the Native American artwork in Crump's cave had been spared from the hands of vandals. Unfortunately, a few of the drawings had been forever scarred by thoughtless intruders. Modern day graffiti was superimposed over these ancient illustrations. Block lettering with sayings such as, "Joe was here," left open wounds of red clay which defaced the ancient ceremonial offerings documented by the Indians centuries ago.

The archaeologists arranged to have several of the glyphs radio-carbon tested in order to establish their age. The material to be tested was small fragments of the charcoal deposits embedded in the glyph walls, left by the charred cane torches which had been stoked into the walls by the ancient cave dwellers. The glyph room was over a mile, deep into the cave, in a remote hard to reach area. To venture this far back in the cave, equipped with only lit cane torches, took skill and courage.

Evidence was building, that the cave appears to have been an authentic Native American sacred ceremonial site. At that point, the archaeologists' were not quite ready to make that determination. The intriguing question kept being asked, why would the cave dwellers traverse so far into the cave, at such risk, to draw symbols at this one specific location? Was this some ceremonial rite of passage imposed on a young man in order to formally attain status

59

with the dwellers? There were other areas in the cave, much closer to the entrance, which could have been used to make drawings. The answer remained a mystery.

The mystique of the cave had become contagious among us. Maybe it was just a romantic notion, that an elusive supernatural force resonated within this cave, guiding and directing the primitive inhabitants toward a higher, more noble purpose, thus the existence of a ceremonial site. Our shared objective, to protect this cave, is further enhanced with the proposition of it being a sacred, ceremonial site of the Indians. This captivating concept was further propelled by the results of the radio-carbon testing.

Four glyph cane torch scrapings had been submitted for analysis. Two of the glyphs carbon tested to around 1400 A.D. The other two specimens were dated to around 30 B.C. The researchers' were astounded! The majority of previous findings established a time span ranging from 900 A.D. to 1700 A.D. Our carbon test date of 30 B.C. identifies glyphs which are almost a thousand years older than any previously documented. Another significant test result was the wide span of the date findings from the four specimens, stretching from 30B.C to 1400 A.D. These findings substantiate ceremonial activities spanning at least1300 years. In essence, ritual cave drawings had been made within the cave for well over a thousand years.

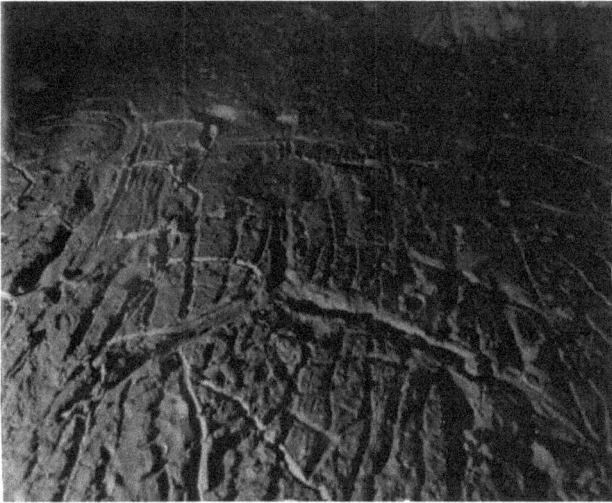

Indian Mud Glyph Known As "Big Momma and Family" Radio Carbon Dated at 30 B.C. *Notice: Modern graffiti letters "B" and "R" on the left of ancient glyph*

There was something very special and unique about this cave, and more specifically the gallery room. Generations of Native Americans preformed the same type ritual, making ceremonial drawings at the same exact location. This is comparable with an analogy to 1300 year old churches and cathedrals in Europe. Any possibility of error had been ruled out. The lab contracted to complete the testing was highly respected and the testing had been repeated multiple times, always with the same result.

In the final analysis the authenticated motif storyboards, document a great spiritual awakening of a nomadic primitive people, which was inspired by nature and captured most vividly in the great cavern. A natural shelter and refuge, which evolved into a Holy sanctuary; set aside for the singular purpose of communion with the Great Spirit that held dominion over all natural phenomena and living things.

During the era of antiquity, nomadic tribes traversed large regions within what is now recognized as the Ohio Valley area. These roaming peoples are accepted to be the first cave dwellers in the karst region; which has an ample number of easily accessible natural caverns. Because these caves were ready-made shelters; many were revisited frequently by nomadic hunting parties. It is reasonable to suppose that long ago it was a hunting party that first entered this cavern.

We can only speculate about what these first cave explorers may have sensed as they walked the ancient passages. Supposing they had a light source such as a hand held torch, did they gaze in awe at the colossal dome of this cavern; and what thoughts were stirred in their minds, as their fingers traced the scalloping of the walls? They were surely overjoyed to find the strong waterfalls, which would provide an abundance of fresh water for the party during their sojourn. There was plenty of floor space for a large group to sit or lay for rest and rejuvenation. I imagine men sitting cross-legged encircling an open fire, as foods were being prepared for cooking at the close of a long day of hunting; while they fashioned spears and arrowheads, making ready for the rising sun of the coming day.

I believe the first impressions of the ancient nomads mirror those of modern day spelunkers, who gaze with reverence at nature's grand display of natural raw beauty.

This cavern is a unique creation formed in total darkness; perfected with a natural order which is shrouded in opulent splendor, strongly suggesting an immeasurably intelligent and omnipresent sovereign designer, who delights in masterful works. How could they not perceive the presence of one deity that is everywhere; who prevails in the light, in the darkness, and in all of nature?

Through the mud glyph record they left of their unrelenting spiritual journey, nothing is left to speculation; it is a certainty that they indeed found within the stone walls of this cave, the Great Benefactor who was mindful of every need and would sustain them in this life and the spirit world beyond.

Chapter IV

Iron Sentinel: Modern Day Good Shepherds

Although today, we seemingly are drowning in a secular world; ancient faith declarations etched on stone walls by a lost culture of a past age, should never become categorized as dead artifacts. To the contrary, these mud glyph testimonials remain as proclamations of a living society of humans; disposed to share their thoughts, values, beliefs, aspirations, and reliance on the Creator with all humanity, even those fixed in a future time beyond the realm of their imaginings. The fortification of these devotional inscriptions must be protected for all perpetuity.

The occurrences of pilfering and looting of Indian artifacts from the cave had been problematic for a long time. More recently the perpetrators ceased to be the occasional local arrowhead collectors; as a black market developed for relics of a seemingly morbid genre, such as human bones and skulls dug-up from the interment sites of Shaman priests. This incursion cast a long ominous aura around this once sacred site; as these thieves generally operated in the shadows as they conducted their vile sacrileges. What was once holy was being defiled.

This growing problem would not relent. So later I met with the archaeologists in order to plan our next move. The professionals stressed to me, as the cave owner, the significance of finding such ancient mud glyph drawings within the cave. They were very concerned about the extreme vulnerability of the glyphs to vandalism.

There had already been some minor degree of damage. The lead archaeologist believed the only solution was to gate the cave opening. Gating had been done at several other caves worthy of protection.

A new gate design, referred to as a "bat gate," had been engineered by Mr. Roy Powers, who had then supervised the installation of several bat gates in the U.S. and South America. The gates are constructed with angle iron, and designed to allow for the bat population to enter and leave their habitat without difficulty. The problem facing us is the very large size of the cave entrance. A gate constructed for this cave would be enormous, and very expensive due to material costs and labor expenditures. The location of the cave offered challenges as well. It is located in a relatively remote location, at the bottom of a two acre, heavily forested sinkhole. All the building materials would have to be carried by hand to the cave entrance. The only other option discussed, was the possibility of erecting a smaller bat gate at the crawl space opening site, which is about a half mile into the cave.

My concern with the alternate recommendation was that the front section of the cave for a half mile would remain unprotected and still defenseless to trespassing vandals. As the cave owner, I believed my stewardship was to protect the entire cave, not solely the Indian mud glyphs.

The main problem we faced was the cost of erecting such a large bat gate, and where we could acquire the funding to undertake this enormous project. The most feasible option was to try and obtain grant capital. We were faced with a long and cumbersome application process which may take several years to fruition, if successful. We were in agreement that the situation was urgent, with this latest significant discovery being unprotected. Dan Davis expressed his concern of the prospect someone may actually try to carve out some of the glyphs, hoping to keep them in tact for sale on the black market. This idea was a horrifying thought, but not outside the realm of possibility. We decided we would have to keep a close watch on the glyph gallery room through daily monitoring of these finds.

Valerie had previously worked as the chief archaeologist with the Kentucky Heritage Council, a state agency responsible for the acquisition, oversight, and preservation of historical properties throughout the commonwealth. The agency has access to some limited grant monies, and she agreed to explore the possibility of securing some of the funding for our project through them. This strategically would be our first step.

In late fall of that year, two members of the Green River Grotto group contacted me concerning an experiment they wanted to conduct at the entrance to the cave. Having studied all the caves in southern Kentucky, they realized Crump's cave was the only one with an entrance having a direct southern exposure. This was a curiosity to them, and they were captivated with the idea that there may be some connection with the southern exposure and the existence of Indian mud glyphs in the cave. No other caves in the area had these drawings, and no other cave had the direct southern entry exposure.

The experiment they proposed related to the winter equinox. In ancient days, time was determined by the location of the stars and the movement of the sun. Sundials were eventually designed as a result of the reliance on the sun's movement for exact time measurement. The cave, with its rare southern exposure, allowed for the entry of sunlight, and more importantly distinctive sun beams or rays. The twenty-first of December is the shortest day of the year, heralding in the ever so gradual daily increase of daylight hours. The tracking of sunlight was the ancient method used to identify the seasons.

The team's plan was to measure the length of the sun's rays penetrating the cave mouth for the entire month of December. The trees stripped of their foliage by this time, allow for the unimpeded entry of sun beams into the cave mouth.

On sunny days, they would set markers at the end of the penetrating shaft of sunlight. The theory being, that if the sun shone on December twenty-first, the light beam cast into the cave, would be at its longest length. The contrast of light cutting through the overwhelming darkness within the cave would be dramatic, making it easy to precisely mark the ending of the penetrating sun rays.

Beginning on the first day of December, and each day through December the thirty-first, members of the grotto group made the measurements, marking the length of the sun's rays intruding into the mouth of the cave, using rocks for markers. Luckily, December first was clear and sunny which allowed for a distinct marking. In all, eighteen of the thirty-one days were sunny to partly sunny.

The study results verified that December the twenty first, had indeed produced the longest measured sun ray. The following two days, December the twenty-second and twenty-third had been too cloudy to permit accurate measurement, but on the twenty- forth the sun's ray measured was shorter, indicative of the retreating sunlight and gradually longer days.

The group theorized that this same process of measuring the sunbeams entering the cave mouth could have been used by the early Native Americans as a type of sun dial. This information would be important to the ancient society, for their very existence.

They were gatherers of foodstuff which was naturally available, provided by Nature. They were also game hunters. They cultivated their own crops of corn and squash. In short, they had total reliance on the land for their subsistence. A reliable signal of an impending change of the season would have been an important event to the Indians. The promise of longer days for hunting, gathering and planting, as the gloom of winter would relent to the warmer days of spring, would have been good news. It is speculated that the inception of the winter equinox brought a time for great celebration.

Archaeological field studies of the above grounds located near the cave, uncovered evidence of a small village occupied by nomads who periodically stayed in the area.

These gatherings most likely were associated with special events such as the winter equinox, wedding parties, tribal worship rituals, and healing ceremonies. Another interesting historical conclusion is that the tribal holy men, often referred to as shamans, actually lived year round at these ceremonial caves, taking a leading role in these celebratory practices.

The mystique of the cave was increased by the

likelihood it had been used as a sacred ceremonial site, with the discoveries of the mud glyphs and now the winter equinox feature, accelerating the sense of urgency to provide protection for this rare, ancient artifact.

Modern man has no inherent understanding of the natural bond the Indians had with this cave for so long. To this early society, the cave was recognized as Mother Earth, embracing its habitants with security, warmth, shelter, pure water, visual beauty, sacred worship ground, and even providing a time piece.

My thoughts once more harkened back to the decision I had made to allow the Green River Grotto members access to the cave for their survey. Their activities had uncovered so many hidden secrets which had been guarded for centuries by this cave. My previous apprehension regarding this decision no longer existed. I had learned so much about this cave that I would never have known, as a result of the exploration and research done by so many with the expertise to expose these mysteries.

Valerie thought we had a decent shot at obtaining a grant through the Kentucky Heritage Council, which would provide the funds needed to erect the bat gate at the cave entrance. She initiated the application process for consideration. The discovery of the rare mud glyphs was our strongest claim for endorsement. Grant monies are quite limited and competition to secure funding is often fierce. It may take a couple of years for the application to make its way through the required red tape.

Meanwhile, we continued to monitor the glyph gallery. At least weekly, volunteers ventured back into the cave to check the glyphs. No evidence of any further damage had been detected. I had set-up more of the motion detectors with the sirens and spotlights at the cave entrance. In addition, tape recorders were placed inside the cave, which were turned on each night. Periodically, the recorder would emit a sound of voices which would echo within the cave, hopefully discouraging any intruders. I eventually removed them, fearing the noises may frighten the bats as they left and reentered the cave nightly. Extra, official looking signs were posted around the property. We were in a holding pattern, awaiting word of our fate from the Kentucky Heritage Council.

The saying, ignorance is bliss, certainly was applicable to our situation. If the survey had not been conducted, there would be no discoveries, no sense of responsibility would exist, thus no worries. However, the pattern of periodic looting would continue indefinitely, slowly destroying this archaeological treasure. Sadly, ten thousand years of prehistoric history had already been abolished.

Surprisingly, I received a call from Valerie later that same winter, advising me that the Kentucky Heritage Council had agreed to fund the construction of the bat gate. The monies allocated would pay for the cost of all the construction materials required, but would not cover labor costs. A sum of $6,500.00 would be provided to the American Cave Conservation Association and the Cave Research Foundation, who would oversee the purchase of the gate materials. Volunteers from the National Speleological Society, The American Cave Conservation Association, and Western Kentucky University would provide the labor. Archaeologists from Eastern Kentucky University, the University of Louisville, the University of Kentucky, as well as other archaeological clubs planned to assist in the construction of the gate.

The grant proposal had called for over a thousand volunteer work hours and six tons of angle iron. The estimated length of the gate was about sixty-eight feet, and ten feet tall at the highest point. When completed, it would be the second longest bat gate in the world, and the longest in the United States in 1994. The bat gate designer, Roy Powers, had agreed to volunteer his time with the grant funds picking up his travel expenses. We were all elated with this news, and eager to begin construction.

The super-fast response to the grant application has to be credited to Valerie Haskins and her close association with the Kentucky Heritage Council. It was remarkable to have received approval for the funding so quickly. Fortunately, the Council had recognized the urgency in protecting this Kentucky time capsule.

During the next two weeks, I received calls from numerous volunteers asking for directions to the cave. We established the first day of construction to begin the first weekend of February. The materials had been delivered by a semi-truck and unloaded at the top of the sinkhole. All the material would have to be carried seven hundred feet down to the cave mouth. The construction schedule was set for the four weekends in February. We estimated approximately one hundred people would be on site every weekend.

Construction day finally arrived. Early that morning, carloads of people began arriving at the farm. I had designated a building just behind the house, to serve as the central gathering place for the volunteers. The building was a one room school house which had been built back in the 1800's. There was a sense of excitement which permeated as the size of crowd grew. The group came from all walks of life; however, most were cavers.

Mr. Power's arrived early that morning coming from Virginia. As the designated leader of the building project, he began organizing the volunteers into various assigned groups. Teams of two began carrying the ten foot long angle iron bars down to the cave. Each team used leather shoulder straps to hoist the bar and begin the trek down the side of the sinkhole to the cave entrance. Each bar weighed over two hundred pounds, requiring young, strong, and stout men to manage the heavy load. The necessary hiking up and down the trail made the effort all the more difficult. Thankfully, the weather conditions were agreeable, particularly for February in Kentucky.

At the actual worksite archaeologists were busy scanning the foundation area for any stray artifacts. A team of welders were setting up their equipment. All gate joints would require welded connections. Two heavy drills had also been transported down to the cave entrance. The drills were needed to create holes in the ceiling rock for mounting iron bars, which would eventually be welded into the holes, anchoring the top angle iron plates.

People were milling around like worker ants, performing their designated tasks. I spotted several members of the original Green River Grotto survey group, here once more, volunteering more of their time, for the preservation and protection of the cave.

That first weekend, much of the time was devoted to accomplishing the preparation work needed, in order to actually commence construction. Some of the volunteers requested permission, with supervision, to venture back into the cave to view the Indian mud glyph gallery. I readily agreed. They certainly had earned the opportunity to see these treasures first-hand. They had committed their time, covering personal expenses themselves, in order to be involved in this undertaking. I wanted them to see just what they were protecting. Small groups of five would be taken back to the glyph room at the conclusion of each work day.

Late Sunday evening, they all departed for home, planning to return the following Friday afternoon. Several of the volunteers, coming from significant distances, and other states, intended to stay overnight the next Friday and Saturday. I offered to let some stay in the schoolhouse, which had bathroom facilities, so with their sleeping bags and a couple of space heaters I could provide, they would be fairly comfortable. Some of the others had planned to stay at a local motel. I contacted the motel manager, who agreed to a special rate for these folks.

The one-room schoolhouse where volunteers stayed overnight during the bat gate construction.
Photo Courtesy of: Dr. Chris Groves

That first week I managed to sleep with one eye open at night, going down to the construction site each day to be certain none of the equipment was disturbed. The bat gate foundation and the first section of bars had been secured during the first weekend of work. Viewing the first phase of the gate actually taking form, I reflected on all these people who were committing their labor, at personal financial cost, to participate in, and be witness to this achievement. I was indebted to these volunteers and held them in high esteem, for their passion to cave preservation.

The second weekend arrived with the construction crew trickling in that Friday evening. This weekend, started off with bitterly cold weather conditions, but no one complained. Even with the space heaters in the schoolhouse, the building was uncomfortably cold. I brought them extra blankets along with plenty of hot coffee and doughnuts, in an effort to make these unpleasant conditions a bit more tolerable.

Working inside the cave actually proved to provide a warmer environment from the elements outside. The constant welding of the angle iron bars actually tended to warm the air immediately inside the cave. By Sunday, the gate had grown in height to five feet, as it developed into the colossal gate barrier which was needed in order to halt the unwelcomed trespassing. The bars of the gate allowed for the exact spacing required to allow for bat movements. A lot of testing had preceded Mr. Power's final design for a bat friendly barricade.

At the end of the second weekend of work, we were right on schedule, and about half way finished with construction. A small entry door with a complex locking design had been assembled, making access into the cave even more restrictive, boosting my level of confidence in the gate's ability to keep out invaders.

By this time, many of the volunteers had seen the Indian mud glyphs. There was a lot of speculation about the possible meanings of the drawings. Of course no one knew with certainty, but the consensus was that they had a spiritual meaning to the cave worshipers. Archaeologists from the University of Kentucky were particularly puzzled by several of the human figures which had the mud dug out from the heads of the forms. The height of conjecture centered on the possibility that the scooped out mud had been taken from the heads of the drawings to be used in ceremonial activities conducted outside the cave. Other bewildering depictions had the appearance of large boats with masts. These drawings are especially perplexing as the cave as we know it, is located so far inland from the sea or large water mass.

We know from historical study, that Spanish explorers' traveled here to the new world early in the seventeenth century and may have encountered some of the Indian tribes. One can only wonder if there is any connection. Similarly, one interesting glyph portrays a drawing resembling a cross. Speculation being that many of these explorers had been missionaries, possibly endeavoring to spread Christianity to this new world. The exact interpretation of the ancient drawings will always remain a mystery; a secret kept harbored within the maze of passageways in the cave.

I sensed the cave's mystique infecting many of these newcomers, increasing their feeling of urgency to complete the barrier of protection for this cave in distress. The spiritual dimension they detected during their visit to the glyph gallery furthered their impatience to accomplish the work.

David Foster, who was affiliated with Hidden River Cave, and the American Cave Conservation Association which had been a driving force in making the gate construction possible, told me to expect a film producer who would arrive the next weekend to do a short documentary about the gate project. He would want to interview me as a part of the film.

Early the following week, I was contacted by Tom Law, an independent film producer in

Cincinnati, Ohio. His company, Pangea Productions, had been designated by the Kentucky Heritage Council to compile the documentary. On Saturday, Mr. Law arrived at the cave, accompanied by two assistants and a lot of heavy duty camera equipment. He advised the volunteer group that he would be filming the work they were doing constructing the bat gate and would be going back to the glyph gallery to capture the art work. He promised to make every effort to not be intrusive.

The production, yet to be accomplished, already had some regional Public Broadcasting Service television entities, expressing interest in airing it in their markets. We scheduled a time on his last day on site, to complete an on camera interview for the film. Some of the volunteers guided him and this crew back to the glyph room, helping transport all the camera equipment. This proved to be no easy feat, as the equipment was heavy and cumbersome. In the lake room, a narrow ledge pathway had to be traversed by side-stepping, to pass around the large body of water, in order to reach the intended destination. If by chance you should slip while maneuvering this narrow path, you and the equipment being carried, would tumble into the lake. All breathed a well-deserved sigh of relief, after making safe passage to and from the art gallery.

Bat Gate
One section of 68 foot long cave gate1994. At that date, the longest cave security gate in the United States and the second longest in the world.

Completed bat gate view from inside cave vestibule. Photo Courtesy of: Dr. Chris Groves

At the conclusion of that third weekend, the estimation was that the work was eighty percent complete. The gate looked awesome, all sixty-eight feet of it! It was very imposing and formidable. I smiled, as I envisioned the shocked expressions which would with certainty; appear on the faces of the middle of the night trespassers, when they first encounter this iron sentinel. The gate was secured to the cave foundation which was solid rock, forbidding any one from slivering underneath. There was no way they could fit through the narrow bar spaces. Just a few inches at the very top of the gate, remained to be closed, and the bat gate would be complete.

One afternoon, venturing down to the gate to admire the handiwork of the volunteers, I realized no one could violate and loot this sanctuary again! I determined this called for a concluding celebration. Turning to leave, a burst of sunlight shone on the very location we suspected had been the ancient burial site, where the trespassers had removed the human skulls in the 1970's. Today this hallowed ground was inside the gate and no longer within the looters grasp. A small sparrow was perched atop the gate. I pondered the thought that the tears streaming down the old man's weathered face, I had imagined at the cave entrance, were no longer tears of pain and distress but rather tears of joy. All now seemed to be right with the world, as the gate and the sparrow stood guard.

The final construction weekend had arrived with much anticipation. The weather was shaping up, looking to be cooperative, as the volunteers began showing up; all looking forward to the completion of the project. The filming crew pulled in and began unloading their equipment. They told me, the documentary would be titled, "Saving a Kentucky Time Capsule," which I thought absolutely captured the theme of this effort.

Late in the day, the final iron pins were welded in place to the top iron plate of the cave ceiling. Following some minor adjustments to the small entry door, the bat gate was completed. The mood had become festive, as the camera people set their lighting backdrop, to film the entire length of the gate. There was a lot of handshaking and hugging going on among the volunteers.

David Foster, the group's leader, had an interesting story he shared with the gathering. He was the manager of the Hidden River Cave, which was located in Horse Cave, Kentucky. This large, wet cave ran underneath the town of

Horse Cave and had been polluted for decades by the factory run-off from the local cheese processing plants. The pollutants had become so bad in the cave, that an offensive odor permeated the downtown business district.

David Foster, in conjunction with the American Cave Conservation Association, in a few short years, cleaned the cave of vast amounts of discarded garbage and trash, as well as halting any further commercial waste discharges. They built a state of the art visitor center and museum at the cave, known as the Hidden River Cave, which is open year round for public cave tours. He concluded his story, with a short speech thanking everyone for their hard work and overall dedication to the cave conservation cause.

Adding my own words of gratitude to the assembly, I invited them to a chili supper at the main house. Enough chili had been prepared for a small army, and most ate heartily. I asked them to sign a guest registry, and issued an open invitation to each to return to visit us and the cave any time. As the sun began setting, they began to leave for home. I knew they each had a great sense of accomplishment regarding their achievement, and would never forget this grand experience. I knew I never would.

Following my interview with Tom Law for the documentary, the film production crew packed up their equipment and said their good-byes. He assured me he would send a copy of the film as soon as it was completed for release.

David Foster went over some tips on how to operate the gate's entry door and suggested some maintenance practices. His final official duty was to give me the gate keys. It was a wonderful feeling, knowing the days of vandals, looters, and trespassers were over. This long and destructive chapter for the cave had come to the end. I would sleep a lot better at night.

A documentary video of the erection of this second longest Iron Cave Gate in the world, and a dialogue with involved archeologists about the ancient mud glyph drawings was produced by the Kentucky Heritage Council in 1994; and aired on PBS television and through various worldwide media outlets. The reader is encouraged to view this informative documentary at: **www.archaeologychannel.org.**Select the video tab; click on Kentucky videos; scroll to Saving a Kentucky Time Capsule.

Bat Gate as silhouetted by the morning sun - 2004

Chapter V

Deliverance Abounds
Entrepreneurship

For the next several months I began focusing on a new business venture of establishing a Bed and Breakfast. The farm property had a long rich history. The house and barns had been built in the mid nineteenth century. The grounds were attractive and the location, so close to Mammoth Cave National Park, made it suitable for such an operation. My thinking being; an overnight stay, combined with a cave tour would present a unique package for visitors to the area who may not be candidates for camping out or staying at a motel.

Years earlier, I had entertained the possibility of converting the cave to a public tour venture. I eventually vetoed that idea, to concentrate all my effort to confront the problem of trespassers and vandalism. Not wanting to deface the natural environment surrounding the cave which would be necessitated with a commercial operation, I felt the limited use of the cave, under a strictly controlled situation, might be a possibility. Guided tours for overnight guests would be manageable.

My first consideration had to be the safety of those I would bring into the cave. No doubt, the public would be interested in the exciting story of the gating of the cave entrance and the unique treasures the gate protected. The first thing to undertake was the installation of electric power in the front seven hundred feet of the cave. It would likely be impossible to venture any further back into the caverns interior; it was too rugged and impervious for benign public access.

The front section of the cave had a wide passageway and high ceilings. My brother-in-law Sonny is an electrical engineer. He and his wife Betty were scheduled to arrive the following month for their annual fall visit. I would take this opportunity to present my plan for the cave with Sonny, knowing he would have invaluable advice on how I should proceed.

Daily, I would venture down to the cave; marveling at the massive iron sentinel standing guard, making a bold statement gleaming in the morning sun. According to the designer, the four inch thick angle iron would last well over a hundred years. Running the full length of each bar was a thick iron rod, placed within the interior, which would prevent any efforts made to torch-cut through the angle iron to obtain illegal entry. No compromises were made in the design and construction of this gate. This was comforting and reassuring.

Walking the center passage, I identified specific strategic locations for the placement of wiring and light fixtures. I wanted to camouflage all the lighting fixtures, wiring, and other metal components as much as possible, in order to sustain the natural atmosphere within the cave. Even before talking with Sonny about my ideas, I knew it would take a considerable amount of electrical equipment to illuminate a cave tour corridor. The cost would be a concern as I was on a limited budget, so installation may need to be done in stages, as funds were available.

The next month we started the project. Sonny's stay in Kentucky would only be about ten days, so we moved quickly. He had worked as an electrical engineer with NASA for many years, a natural perfectionist; he effortlessly outlined the plan so every aspect would be executed with great care and precision. We began with the running of electric lines for five hundred feet, starting just inside the bat gate and moving inward. By the end of the first week, we had completed the installation of lighting for this first five hundred feet of the cave interior.

Switching on the power to this area for the first time was very exciting. Before now, flashlights had only given us a tantalizing hint as to what may be seen. As the burst of thousands of watts of light totally eradicated the stark darkness of this section of the cave, the natural beauty of its interior became entirely exposed, as it had never been before. It was a breathtaking sight!

In a couple of days, our visitors left to return to their home in Florida. We had accomplished a lot in a short time. The project would have to be placed on hold until they returned the following fall.

Bill Marohnic checking cave walkway
Photo Courtesy of: Dr. Chris Grove

Sonny, being a professional engineer, was methodical and exacting in his approach to all things. I had witnessed other experts' demeanors, initially shrouded with a scientific indifference, having become infected by the mystique of this cave; ultimately surrender to an emotionally created need to offer protection. Sonny was not different. I had known him for thirty years. I could see subtle changes in his attitude as if unfolding, into a more softened and nurturing relationship with the cave.

Having seen this occurrence so many times, with so many people over the years, I began to refer to it as the cave mystique. I had heard others say the cave was casting a spell. Whatever this intangible enigma was, it had fostered tangible results, such as the gating of the cave. I knew it to be real, as I had become infected almost at the moment I first visited the cave.

I now turned my attention to the various nature trails within the two acres surrounding the cave entrance. Nature had increased its grip with a bountiful display of wild flowers, tangling honeysuckle vines, and wild rose bushes, which produced sweet perfumed breezes. After a bit of pruning, I began building narrow wooden walkways and little bridges, along the trails, among the vast floral display. Our future guests would enjoy early morning and evening walks, along these paths which provided a great opportunity for bird watching. I placed occasional benches along the trails as momentary shade respites. This would be a nice sanctuary for guests seeking escape from the fast lane and a reconnection with nature.

By this time I had received the DVD from Tom Law, which had been contracted by the Kentucky Heritage Council, on the construction of the bat gate. Three episodes were included on the disc, the third being the documentary about the cave titled, "Saving a Kentucky Time Capsule." The story highlights the discovery of the Indian mud glyphs which lead to the gating project. The narrative and cinematography is first class. For a nominal charge, the DVD could be purchased at the <u>Kentucky Heritage Council.com</u> website. In coming years, we would sell copies of the DVD at the Bed and Breakfast. For many guests, this was a unique memento for them to take home, commemorating their stay with us.

With the release of the documentary on the internet, as well as several P.B.S. markets, word spread throughout the archaeological network. University inquiries continued, seeking permission for field studies of the mud glyphs. However, I continued to restrict all research activities to Western Kentucky University, and to a lesser degree, the University of Kentucky. The cave remained closed to all caving clubs.

The department of Geology at Western, proposed a water testing project on two of the waterfalls within the cave. The study would determine the degree of pollutants in the water, which would be tracked and monitored on a long term basis, measuring agricultural toxins leeching into the cave, ninety feet above from ground level. The study would provide analysis to aid the farming community in more efficient methods for use, which would reduce ground water contamination. This research would not disturb the established endangered bat colonies residing deep within the cave. I agreed to the project, which was headed by Dr. Chris Groves and the Hoffman Institute. The research project was scheduled to start in about thirty days.

Meanwhile, having completed work on the hiking trails, I moved inside the cave, preparing walkways for public touring. Eventually, the cave walkways would provide safe footing and be marked with lit floodlights. In the coming fall, Sonny and I would finish the lighting, which would total about a thousand liner feet of well-lit path.

The Bed and Breakfast would be open for guest bookings in the fall as well. All guests would have the opportunity to experience the cave tour, as a part of the cost of their room. This was a unique tourist package, as no other lodging options in the cave country, included a cave tour with the stay. Nicholas and I would be the tour guides, as we had previously discussed.

The iconic cross natural cave formation forty feet above cave floor.

Bed and Breakfast guests participating in cave tour
Photo Courtesy of: Dr. Chris Groves

I received an interesting telephone call from a wildlife artist who had seen an airing of "Saving a Kentucky Time Capsule" on P.B.S. He was intrigued by the Indian mud glyphs and wanted to paint a mural which would be a to-scale version of the drawings. This was something I needed to give some thought to, so I told him I would consider his proposal and get in touch with him within a few days.

I made some inquiries and learned that he was well known throughout the state as a Native American painter and sculptor. I was in the process of converting an outbuilding into a small visitor center, and a wall mural depicting the cave drawings, may spark interest and discussion with our Bed and Breakfast guests. There would be no way that the public could actually view the gallery room in the cave, so this type art display might be a second best option.

I called him back and we scheduled a time to meet at the farm to discuss the possibility further. He was eager at this invitation and planned to bring some of his artwork examples for me to see.

The artist, known as "Caveman", arrived at the farm about a week later. He had a strong

English accent and was quite colorful. He wanted to go back to the gallery room to examine the glyphs, assuring me he was an experienced caver and reasonably capable of making the trip. I was not agreeable to the idea of him making the trek on his own, so I told him I would arrange an expedition date for him to visit the gallery room with a member of the Green River Grotto group.

Caveman arrived the following Saturday with his camera equipment. Terry Davis, one of the grotto members, had agreed to guide him that day back to view the mud glyphs. Entering the cave, Terry told me to expect them back by 7:00 p.m.

They were still in the cave at 8:00 p.m. and I started to worry a bit. At 11:00 p.m. I responded to a knock on the door; it was Terry, obviously upset. Caveman was not with him. Terry explained that he had told the artist it was time to shut things down, and leave the cave. They had spent about eight hours in the gallery room and Caveman had taken several pictures of the drawings. Caveman wanted to stay all night in the cave and Terry had made it clear they needed to leave.

The artist refused to cooperate and they continued to argue. Finally, Terry was forced to leave him. The artist assured Terry he was an experienced caver, and when he finished he would leave on his own. Terry was upset by all this, and apologized for just leaving him in the cave, but he needed to get home. I certainly understood the predicament Terry was placed in.

Now I was justifiably worried about the artist. His being alone in the cave, presented all kinds of possible problems. He could get injured, fall into a deep pit, lose his lighting, and even get lost. I went to bed, unable to sleep as I worried about the artist. About 3:00 a.m. there was a banging sound at the door. When I opened it, there stood Caveman, covered with mud and breathing hard. He began expounding the reasons he needed to stay longer in the cave, and he needed to collect as many pictures of the drawings from various angles as possible. However, around 1:00 a.m. he began to feel uncomfortable. Periodically, a few bats would fly by, and he swore he began hearing noises which were spooking him. Eventually, the cave atmosphere overwhelmed him and he decided it was time to leave just as quickly as he could.

My initial irritation with him and his antics was replaced with relief that he had made it out of the cave safely, unhurt. He was eager to leave, explaining he could not wait to get back to his studio and develop the pictures he had taken of the ancient Indian drawings. He would call me later, so we could decide what the next step would be. I was equally eager to get some sleep.

At our next meeting, we discussed the painting of the mural which would be done using the pictures of the glyph drawings he had made. The paintings would be the actual size of the drawings, so would require four foot by eight foot panels, making a sixty foot liner wall presentation. When completed, the wall mural would be dramatic.

Caveman arrived in the early spring at the new visitor center, ready to launch his painting of the mural. I had installed track lighting on the ceiling with small spotlights illuminating the mural panels. Pleased with the format for his art, he began work. Being an eccentric artist, he insisted I not look at the painting until it was totally completed. Humoring him, I let him have all the privacy he needed. He was hard working, spending twelve and fourteen hour days, creating the work.

I was able to compensate him somewhat for his effort, but at a lesser amount than the going rates for working artists. I agreed to publically credit him for the piece and display his business cards to the tourist groups visiting with us. The day arrived when he was ready to present his completed work. As I entered the visitor center, he switched on the track lighting and suddenly there appeared Indian mud glyph reproduction paintings filling the entire room. So well done, they almost appeared to be the real thing, the dark brown background shaded with a green patina hue.

Each four by eight panel depicted a specific glyph. The big momma, an obviously pregnant woman with several children at her side, and the turtle, eagle and snake, popped out as I slowly scanned the mural. The other geometric symbols also pleased the eye. The representation in its entirety, stirred my emotions, as I once again contemplated what the symbolic meaning of each could possibly be. I was extremely pleased with the results; this artwork would leave a lasting impression with those touring the cave, giving them the opportunity to see a representation of the glyph treasures without risking a compromise to the original drawings' integrity or security. The mural also provided a lasting tribute to the actual glyphs, memorializing them.

Fall arrived, ushered in with bold splashes of autumn colors and cooler, more comfortable days. Sonny and Betty were scheduled to arrive soon. I worked feverishly, gathering the supplies needed to finish the electrical work in the cave. The Bed and Breakfast was open and ready for guest bookings. The visitor center with its gallery of Indian mud glyph paintings was complete. The hiking nature trails were awaiting use by visitors. The only project left unfinished was the completion of the cave wiring. This was an exciting time for us.

This final stage of electrical instillation would prove to be more challenging. The area we would be working in was the huge canyon room, with its sixty foot high ceiling and deep central pit. There would have to be some climbing and scaling of the rock walls. It was going to take five hundred feet of wiring to finish the job.

Sonny was impressed with the design of the gate, especially the bat friendly feature. As we began our electrical work, Sonny's experience many years ago as a power lineman, became invaluable. He was able to scale the cave walls with proficiency. Being an electrical expert, he knew precisely where to attach the fixtures and wiring. Setting up the electrical connections and junction boxes where far beyond my abilities, but was basic to him, as an engineer having worked on NASA space rockets.

Following a full week of electrical work, the final connection was made. We had been working in semi-darkness and were eager to throw the switch for the first time.

Turning off our flashlights, which left us in absolute darkness, he flipped the switch. Light flooded the room exposing a glorious sight! Our initial impression was the sheer size of the room. The flood lights in the room captured a small water fall I had not seen before. The narrow stream of water originated at the apex of the huge dome ceiling.

From a certain vantage point, looking back toward the cave entrance, it created the illusion of a sliver of daylight illuminating the cascading water. It was a spectacular visualization. This section would be as far back into the cave tourists would be allowed to go. I was very pleased with the result of all our work, and eager for our guests to see the natural wonders in the cave.

Later that fall, we introduced the public to the cave, through hour long tours. The response was very positive; visitors being most impressed with the massive size of the rooms and passages.

Before spring, I intended to further improve the walkway in the cave. Most commercial cave operations in the area resorted to concrete walks and stairs. I wanted this cave to retain its natural pristine ambiance, so I decided on a rustic looking, wood walkway with handrails which would extend some six hundred feet into the cave. I elevated the structure about six inches off the actual cave floor which placed it high enough to discourage people from picking up rocks and other naturally occurring cave materials. The main cave artery had a scattering of bone fragments, most likely of animal origin, that I did not want to be disturbed.

I employed a construction company to install the walkway. I had chosen arsenic free treated wood for use in the cave in order to reduce the toxin footprint. When the walkway was complete, I studied it with mixed feelings. On one hand, it made touring the cave easy, plus encouraged the group to remain cohesive, minimizing wandering. The introduction of such a large man-made imprint in this natural setting, proved to be a nagging concern for me. I had to rationalize my decision of allowing public access to the cave.

In an effort to make the cave tours even more interesting for our guests, I researched everything I could find regarding the farm or the cave. Western Kentucky University had a vast archive of local historical information which I used extensively. I uncovered evidence that the cave was used in the 1860's as a shelter for runaway slaves using the underground railroad which ran through this section of Kentucky. The Kirby families owned the cave during this period of history, and were known abolitionists. Many slaves passed through this area in their quest to reach the Ohio River which would transport them northward toward freedom. The cave provided a natural respite, with food and extra clothing provided to the runaways by the Kirby's.

The cave was also used by the Kirby family to hide their prized horses, breeding bulls, and fine china prior to Union troop raids which were done on prosperous farms and plantations during the Civil War. Archaeologists' found considerable amounts of broken china and fine dishware in the vestibule of the cave.

Two decades later, in the 1880's, the Crump family used the cave as a major source of water for their farming and personal needs. A 1907 newspaper article featured the cave's elaborate water plant which piped pure cave water to a large collection tank near the main house. This constant water source supplied the family's needs as well as the livestock. During times of severe drought, the farm always had a reliable source of cave water. In these times, residents of the nearby town of Smiths Grove would obtain emergency supplies of water from the Crump's. Many of the water system artifacts remain within the cave, left by the early settlers. All of these visual remnants are pointed out and encourage discussion with guests touring the cave. The large cedar water barrels are still in place with the original pipes connected to the two large waterfalls.

The availability of water in the cave, also served as the backdrop to a small whiskey distillery which was operated inthe1890's.

As a result of my effort to unravel the history of the cave and antebellum home on the property, I was able to secure appointment to the National Register of Historic Places in 1994. The farm is also recognized on the listing of Kentucky Historical sites.

Over the following years, public tours of the cave were mostly limited to the guests of the Bed and Breakfast business. I was approached on several occasions, by business investors encouraging further commercialization of the cave, which would include a tour back to the Indian mud glyph gallery. Each time I contemplated these suggestions, I envisioned a circus like environment, which I could not accept. Some members of the family saw the commercial expansion as the future. No question, the additional financial security an expanded operation may provide, was a tantalizing consideration. However, such development would not guarantee success. Some of the established commercial cave operations were struggling to remain open.

The people who had toured the cave always would tell me before leaving how impressed they were that the natural cave environment had remained untouched for the most part. One old timer told me that this cave reminded him of his first tour as a young boy of Mammoth Cave, many, many years ago. He advised me to leave the cave in its primitive state, thus making it unique from all the others.

I had no confusion about limiting public access to the most beautiful sections of the cave, which were at least a mile within the interior. This was the heart of the cave, which provided protection for the endangered bat colonies, sustained the blind fish in the perfect deep blue waters in the lake room, and safeguarded the ancient mud glyphs. I was secure with my conviction that this section of the cave was considered to be sacred ground by the ancient inhabitants. Since the gating of the cave, this area had been highly restricted to human traffic.

A group of biologists from the state routinely conduct bat census studies, reporting gradual increases in the bat populations and an emergence of a bat nursery and bachelor colony. Preventing the unwelcomed intrusion of trespassers from these habitat areas has resulted in a reversal of the previously declining numbers of endangered bats. Our guests marvel at the lack of mosquitoes at the farm.

I wanted to share the wonders of this historic property with youngsters and make it a place that would be family friendly. In order to do so, we had two cabins constructed; both located in the wooded section just above the hiking trail to the cave entrance.

The first cabin built has two stories; with a large upstairs bedroom and a living room, kitchen, and bathroom on the first floor. We call it the "Little House in the Woods" cabin. It's very comfortable for a family group of four to five. Just as the construction was near completion, I located an historic 1830 log cabin in northern Barren County, only about twenty five miles east of the farm.

The old log home was located near the back section of a large dairy farm and had at one time been the home place for early settlers to south central Kentucky. The first time I saw the house, the logs had been covered over with wood siding. This was likely done in the 1920's or 1930's. The numerous coats of white paint were badly chipped and faded, which emphasized the abandonment this home had endured. This house had been purchased by a couple of local fellows who had established a business of buying, selling, and relocating old historic log cabins. They were seeking a prospective buyer and I could see the possibilities this abandoned homestead would afford my operation; so we struck a deal.

Surprisingly, the structural aspects of the cabin were exceptionally preserved. The doors, the wood plank floors, the staircase, and the porch were all in decent shape. The huge logs, which had been fashioned by hand with an axe, were all straight and sturdy; enduring the passage of time, and the seasons of Kentucky weather to which they had been exposed. We set a date for the log cabin to be dismantled and moved to the farm.

The foundation had been completed and awaited the arrival of the historic cabin. The entire moving process was very labor intensive. Each log was numbered as to its location in the structure, so each log could be placed exactly where it belonged as the cabin was being reassembled. The same scenario with numbering the floor planks, the staircase, etc. It was entirely dismantled, loaded on a large flatbed semi-truck and brought to its new home in Warren County.

Once at the new location site, the reassembly commenced in the reverse. Everything was matched-up; the logs properly dove-tailed, the floors, the doors, and the porch; all original to the cabin as it had been built in 1830.In fact, most of the old hand- forged square head iron nails had been recovered. There were enough of these antique nails to completely fill two five-gallon buckets. It took them a week or so to finish. Then we were left to do the chinking between the logs and add electric wiring, plumbing, and other modern upgrades. Once completed, the cabin had two large bedrooms upstairs, a bathroom, a large kitchen and a living room downstairs. There is plenty of room for a family of six or eight people. We refer to this cabin as the "Historic Pioneer Log Cabin."

The cabins are situated directly above the entrance to the cave and close to the nature trails. Both cabins have large rear decks which overhang the cliff drop off. These lodgings have become ideal for families, cave lovers and nature enthusiasts.

Everything is as it should be. I have limited any further commercial growth, thus insuring the integrity of the property for the enjoyment of nature lovers' and history buffs'. Best of all, the decades old problem with cave vandals and looters no longer exists. Very important university research, designed to improve future environmental conditions, continues to be developed for testing in the cave.

Antebellum Bed & Breakfast House

I hit a pretty big bump in the road as I turned fifty-five. I was diagnosed with diabetes and high blood pressure, forcing me to face the stark reality of my own mortality. Both of my children, now adults, had moved away to other states, pursuing their own dreams. With these life changes, I began to think about the future of the cave. I knew, eventually the property would change ownership, and the historic house would likely be treasured by others. The cave was another matter.

Over the years, I had a passion to be a responsible steward of the cave. I never really considered myself its owner; just an overseer, in line with others of the past and many others yet to come. I wondered what kind of stewardship a future owner would deliver for the cave.

I felt a responsibility to all the individuals and

organizations who had stepped up to rescue the cave. However, some day my family would sell the farm, and new owner's may be faced with the temptation to exploit the cave through disregard or commercialization, which could reverse all that had been accomplished through the efforts of so many. My inclination was to not dwell on this possibility, and just push it to the recesses of my mind, but I knew this issue would eventually demand resolution.

It had been hard to accept that it was time for my children to move on with their lives, and I felt much the same way about the cave. Over the years, the cave and I had bonded; it had grown on me, becoming increasingly important in my life. I had a similar protective instinct for its future that as a parent, I had for my kids. The major geologic and archaeological features within the cave, along with its Native American heritage, befit special care and attention regarding its future welfare. I cannot take this responsibility lightly.

As the months passed, I had not reached any acceptable resolution as to how the future could be made secure for the cave. On the day following my sixty-first birthday, I read an article about a local landowner placing a three hundred acre hardwood forest into protective status with the state. According to the piece, the forest contained several endangered plants and wildflowers. These species were extremely rare and close to extinction. The landowner had received compensation from the state for placing the acreage into a protective status. This action had been prompted as a result of competing commercial interests making offers on the timber; the harvesting of which would eradicate the small plant life within the forest, including the endangered flora. The landowner decided to sell the property to the state, taking a financial loss, but saving the old trees so his grandchildren could enjoy them. State ownership would allow his family to use trails within the forest for hiking. To me, this seemed like a perfect example of stewardship.

The concept of the cave, someday becoming a state protected property, intrigued me. However, the thought of losing my twenty year tenure as steward, brought on a feeling of dread. I realized this was a somewhat selfish emotional reaction on my part, which was not necessarily in the best interest of the cave. When discussing this with the family, their reaction initially was the same as mine. The thought of parting with the cave just did not resonate. The cave was special to them as a family property, filled with wonderful memories spanning two decades. I knew I would need to give this a lot of thought; weighing the pros and cons. My natural inclination was to procrastinate and make no decision, one way or the other.

Fate intervened a few days later, when Dr. Groves stopped by to discuss his research work in the cave. He and his associates with the Hoffman Environmental Research Institute, a subsidiary of the geology department at Western, had been conducting water research in the cave for several years. This arrangement was revisited annually, so Dr. Groves was here to secure my agreement to another year of study.

I appreciated the fact that the research Dr. Groves and his group conducted in the cave was meaningful and relative to improving agricultural practices. I also was impressed with their professionalism and respect for the cave, so signing the twelve month extension agreement was an easy decision. As we lingered on the front porch drinking a glass of iced tea, I brought up the article I had read earlier about the timberland which had been purchased by the state becoming a nature preserve. He was aware of the sale and familiar with the agency overseeing such acquisitions.

The agency was the Kentucky Heritage Land

and Conservation Board. Their mission is to award funding for the purchase and preservation of selected natural areas in the state with the goal to protect rare, endangered species, as well as migratory birds.

They are also mandated to save threatened areas of natural importance. Funds are provided through the state; one source being the $10.00 fee charged to individuals electing to purchase Kentucky nature license plates for their vehicles. The board can award grant monies to acquire areas of natural significance in need of protection to local governments, state colleges and universities, as well as to specific state agencies.

Dr. Groves thought the cave may qualify for consideration, as a natural habitat that includes rare and endangered species; the bat colonies meeting that criteria. He told me he would investigate the possibility further. As he left, I once again started to have some anxiety in even broaching the prospect; in part I would be happy to just drop the idea. Yet deep inside, I had the feeling it was important to pursue further inquiry.

Within a few weeks, Dr. Groves met with me to explain what he had learned from the Heritage Land Board. If I was serious in a decision to sell the cave, Western Kentucky University would make application, being the sponsoring governmental agency, and they would ultimately become the legal steward over the cave. They would be required to submit an annual report to the Kentucky Heritage Land Board, insuring they were meeting all aspects of the Board's mission criteria.

There would need to be agreement on a purchase price for the section of the cave on my property, which included the only entrance. The Board would conduct a site visit in order to conclude their intent to proceed with the application. Assuming there was agreement on a purchasing price, and all other conditions were met, they would purchase the property placing it under the legal stewardship of the university. At that point, the university would oversee all aspects of maintaining and protecting the cave. Dr. Groves, a professor with the Geology Department at Western, and Director of the Hoffman Environmental Institute, along with many graduate and under graduate students would conduct all research activities and insure security for the cave.

At first I was not inclined to sell the two forested acres adjacent to the cave entrance, which included the nature trails. However, this property would not enjoy the protection as a state property, leaving its future unsettled. In due course I realized the forest area should be included with the cave sale, placing both properties in protected status for all perpetuity. This limited the possibility of the stately old trees ever falling under the ax.

The wooded two acres are unique as a wildlife habitat. Many of the plants near the cave entrance are conserved in a micro-climate maintained by the temperature and humidity factors unique to the environment of the cave mouth. On hot summer days, cool and refreshing air emanating from the cave entrance, lowers the air temperature for several feet, some twenty to thirty degrees. Conversely, in the deep chill of winter, warm air bellows form the cave mouth, warming the immediate outside air significantly. No wonder the Native Americans depended on the shelter provided by the cave, year round.

The emerging possibility of placing the cave in protective status weighed heavily on my mind. I must confess, that over the years, my efforts to commercialize the cave, even on a limited basis, did not feel right. The fact that the cave was an ancient ceremonial site which included burial grounds, revered by generations of tribal societies, seemed out of step with current day public touring by vacationing motorists. Somehow I felt the Native elders of long ago, would be very displeased with the activities occurring at the cave today.

I recalled a strange incident which occurred a few months ago. We had a couple of weeks of very stormy weather that had caused some minor damage at the farm. I went down to the nature trail to access the cave for flooding. As I proceeded down the path, I was stopped by a medium sized tree that had fallen which blocked the rail. There were broken limbs everywhere, making passage difficult. Deciding to take an alternate route, I found a second tree which had fallen, blocking the way. The only remaining trail to the cave was longer, but I proceeded on that path, only to be stopped short by another, much larger tree, which had fallen preventing passage. These were the only trees which had been downed by the high winds of the storm. Making my way back to the house to arrange for a clean-up crew, I wondered if this was a sign; a message from Mother Nature to get my attention.

My rational thinking dismissed this idea, as I considered the many conversations I had with numerous karst scientists over the years.

Geologists, who studied the cave, have precise scientific explanations as to how the cave formation occurred. Archaeologists, who have examined the many cave artifacts, have pieced together a mosaic of ancient tribal civilizations and cultures. These disciplines provide the study of physical properties that give us much information about ancient times. However, there are metaphysical facets that do not lend themselves to scientific inquiry. These aspects remain elusive, even mysterious and defy explanations or measurement. For example, many people have told me that after visiting the cave, they felt a definite energy, which made a lasting impression on them. The cave's primeval history as a ceremonial and burial site may be responsible for the special cave mystique, I have often mentioned. I have witnessed the cave's charisma permeate individuals, acting almost like a contagion within the groups associated with the various cave projects, infusing a collective cave rescue mentality which infects to a near obsessive level.

Detached cave scientists become impassioned cave rescuers. They maintain their professionalism, but with added focus and urgency. Those with a more poetic nature, say the cave casts a spell. We are left to wonder. We can state with certainty, "it" remains elusive and unexplained; impossible to define or capture. Similar to many of life's experiences that we can only attribute to fate or coincidence; which end up being of vital personal importance, sometimes altering life directions.

Of all the features of the cave that resonate with me, the fact that it was a burial site has the most importance. One day as I was taking my Bed and Breakfast guests to tour the cave, a man approached seeking permission to join the group. He explained that he was a shaman priest of the Chickasaw tribe. He knew of the many standard ancient burial practices used by multiple tribes which habited this region long ago. He told me that often, the tribe shaman, or holy men, lived in or near designated ceremonial caves, responsible for protecting the sacred sites. He believed a cave this size would have been used many generations by the tribal groups. At their death, the shamans were often buried at the cave entrance; in the belief their spirits would continue to protect the consecrated site from intruders. That would possibly explain the burial site which was located at this cave entrance. I could not bring myself to tell him about the skulls that had been removed by looters.

At the conclusion of the tour, my guests departed and the old holy man hung back, lingering just outside the cave mouth. He asked if he might perform a brief ceremony to bless the cave. I was eager to witness this ancient ritual, so we once again entered the cave vestibule. From a well-worn leather pouch, the shaman produced a small bundle of dried sage which he placed reverently upon the face of a flat smooth rock.

I had read that all ceremonies, tribal or private, must be entered into with a good heart, so one could walk in a sacred manner, and be helped by the spirits to enter the sacred realm. Native people throughout the world use herbs to accomplish this. Sage is burned to drive out bad spirits, feelings, or influences, and also to keep bad spirits from entering the area where the ceremony takes place.

When he was satisfied the sage was properly placed he lit the bundle. As the sage began burning, releasing a faint sweet aroma as the thin ribbon of smoke slowly arose toward the high ceiling, the holy man stood up, turning to face the back of the large atrium, and extending his arms upward in praise, ever so gradually turning full circle as he spoke, he began reciting the words of an ancient Indian prayer, known as the ***Blessing and Thanks to the Four***

Directions. His deep voice reverberated throughout the vestibule,

"To the North, whose wise cold wind keeps us humble. To the East, rising sun and the spring of new life.

To the South, whose warm winds bring us abundance.

To the West, whose inspiration motivates us to seek the Kingdom. To Grandfather God, the Creator of all that is seen and unseen.

To Mother Earth, who provides us with all we need; clothing, food, and shelter."

When he had finished, he bowed his head momentarily in silence, just as the sage had been consumed by the fire. As he left me, and slowly climbed the nature trail toward the highway, I knew that he somehow was aware of the desecration that had been thrust upon the cave, without me speaking a word about it. I pondered what force had brought this shaman to the cave that day, and the significant impact this moving, ancient Indian rite seemed to be having on me.

So it became decision time for the family. Personally, I had been caught in the midst of an emotional tug-of-war. I kept thinking of the many people who had come to the rescue of this cave during the past twenty years. Without their interventions, the cave would be near its abyss. Vandals and looters would have ravaged the last remnants of a ten thousand year old depository of American Indian culture; leaving a legacy of a big hole in the ground littered throughout with empty beer cans. However, many individuals in many different ways have left an enduring noble legacy, which is permanently symbolized by the iron sentinel, standing guard.

There was some suggestion to post pone a decision of this magnitude for a later time. There was no need to decide now. I realized that funding to purchase the cave may not be available in the future. Also, there was a slim possibility that university sponsorship could be withdrawn. A temporary window of opportunity was open for a limited time, and it may not appear again. Hesitation may preclude the cave ever being placed in a state protective status. I knew it was up to me to persuade the reluctant family members to agree to the sale.

Working through Dr. Groves, the Heritage Conservation Board and I came to an agreement on the price for the cave and the two acres surrounding its entrance. It was further agreed that our family would have access to the cave on a limited basis, with notification to the university. Also, the nature trails could continue to be used by the family and our Bed and Breakfast guests as long as we own the farm.

The family eventually accepted these terms and we committed to transfer ownership to the state. Placing the cave into a state protective status would soften the personal impact for each family member. We knew our decision would have a long reaching, permanent impact in protecting this cave we all loved so much. Long after we are gone, the imprint of our time as stewards will remain. That will be our legacy.

Pioneer Log Cabin – Circa 1830.
Reassembled at Cave Spring Farm in 2004.
Overnight lodging for cave guests.

"Little House in the Woods" Cabin.

Chapter VI

Horse Rescue!

Farm life presented the opportunity for a former city boy to keep a few pets. A variety of animals over time became members of our family. We had a couple of dogs, two or three cats, a scattering of chickens, a pair of geese, and a cow.

At age fifty, without much forethought, I decided to buy a horse. I have to admit that at this stage in my life it was more of a romantic notion rather than a well thought out plan. I knew very little about horses, but believed I could learn and grow through a trial and error process. I would soon find out just how true that concept was to become.

Taking on the job of caring for a thousand pound animal with an attitude actually never entered my mind. I assumed a horse to be much the same as cows or sheep; rather docile and daft. That thinking was entirely naïve.

To begin with young, unbroken horses are very smart and set in their ways; determined to become the barnyard boss. One soon learns you are to be engaged in a daily power struggle with a half-ton muscular, perceptive, strong- willed athlete that loves to throw its resolve and weight around. With this new insight I understood I had become a student in the "School of Hard Knocks" in my pursuit of the fine points on horse husbandry. I forged ahead, long on enthusiasm and short on smarts. My first projects were building a horse barn and fencing pastures. My family and I owned a small farm with a pre-Civil War historic home that functioned as our home place and a Bed and Breakfast operation. Adding horses I thought, would further advance the theme of offering the

Bed and Breakfast guests an escape from the stress of modern day living by fashioning an old world antebellum momentary trip back in time to the enchantment of a slower era.

One day in late winter, ground was broke for the new horse barn. I recruited a couple of local carpenters to oversee the construction. Although they seemed to be a bit rough around the edges, they assured me they could construct a top-notch barn. Both were perpetual tobacco chewers' and very colorful gents who were just brimming over with an unlimited repertoire of vocal vernaculars. Their scarcity of social etiquette did not cause me much distress since I was not escorting them to a church social. My only concern was that they do a good job building the barn, show-up to work when expected and put in an honest day of labor; which they did.

The barn began to take shape. It was to be modest in size, with three horse stalls and a hay and feed room; constructed of wood and painted white. Dutch barn doors trimmed in red were added, along with a dark red metal roof. A cupola at the center of the roof top was decorated with a fancy weather vane.

I personally built the stall enclosures, dug all the holes for the fence posts, and erected the wood plank fencing which was then finished off with a double coat of white paint. The project was concluded by early spring and we were all pleased with a job well-done. Being only a couple of part time carpenters' and an absolute greenhorn, we probably surprised everyone in the community, by pulling it off.

When complete it was quite handsome; a barn which could be easily seen on any clear morning from a distance of a mile in all directions.

My second project would soon begin. The first spring horse auction would be held in about a month. I was eager to attend. Until then, I would study-up on horse ownership. Following three weeks of reading I realized how little I knew; accepting my limitations I hoped I would learn what I needed "on the job" as I had done with the barn building and fencing.

As the days grew closer to auction day, I admit I began to have a few nagging doubts as to how this would all workout. Would the end result meet my equestrian fantasies or would it all become a comedy of errors? The truth turned out to be somewhere in the middle.

The big day finally arrived! With much excitement and anticipation my son, Nick and I arrived at the livestock complex where the auction was to be conducted. We had gotten there a couple of hours early in order to look around, as if we knew what we were doing. This was our first horse auction and we did not know exactly what to expect and more importantly if we would find a suitable horse or go home empty-handed.

The auction compound was quite large. Pick-up trucks hauling horse trailers were motoring about everywhere and there was constant commotion of new arrivals pulling up to one of the many livestock docks to unload, as others were attempting to pull-out and begin the search for a parking spot. People were milling about everywhere appearing to be tending to business.

As we found our way to the back of the stock yard we were met with a blast of hot air intense with a mingling of such barnyard stench as animal urine and manure along with immense clouds of cigarette smoke, all combined creating a foggy, steamy haze. Unaccustomed to such a concentration of pungent odor it was grotesque to our senses, but no one else around seemed to even notice. What appeared to be hundreds of horses, mules, goats, and some hogs were all penned in an area together, barely able to move around.

We climbed a flight of stairs which took us up to a large cat-walk above the sea of anxious and frightened animals. They seemed to sense their dilemma; all in unfamiliar surroundings they appeared to share a mounting collective fear of the unknown and what would be the end of all this.

No question, there was the atmosphere of a gigantic marketplace with wheeling and dealing taking place in the shadows, kids running around, food smells intermingling with the odors of human sweat and tobacco. It brought to my mind the base inhumanity and cruelty directed to some of these animals as I observed the occasional stockyard worker kicking and whipping some of the unruly, panicked captives. This was a rude awakening for me, actually seeing what I considered to be the seedy side of the livestock market business. This thought crossed my mind, was I here to buy a horse or to rescue it? I preferred to focus on the buying aspect; just a simple cash transaction in without any sob stories. I had seen all I wanted to of the back stage or underbelly of animal auctions.

The auction began suddenly and one horse at a time was paraded into the viewing arena. The auctioneer was perched in a booth enclosure above the ring, microphone in hand he rapidly introduced each animal as he provided scant background information, getting right to the bidding in a rapid fire manner. Each transaction took only about five minutes as those bidding would raise a numbered card which noted their recorded identification with the stockyard business office.

The guy sitting next to me pointed out a fellow he identified as the "X buyer" who was bidding on many of the horses which looked rough, lame or old. These horses were drawing only very low bids. The X buyer was acquiring horses for a glue factory, thus a certain death warrant was issued to each horse he purchased. I suppose the owners of these horses believed them to be "used up" so they were now undesirable, yet they were intent on getting some final meager monetary pay-out from the animal. It was sad to watch them being led out of the arena unaware of their imminent fate. As the auction continued, I became somewhat fixated on the bidding of the X buyer, secretly feeling relieved if another buyer out bid him and liberated a horse from his lethal grasp.

It was getting to be late in the day and the crowd began to thin out. I was starting to lose hope that I would find a horse to my liking at this auction. The entire experience was becoming a huge disappointment which could be summed up as another demonstration of man's greed and cold-heartedness, as about half of the horses auctioned so far were doomed for slaughter following a long hot day absent of feed or water. The only measure of kindness I witnessed was water misting of the animals as they awaited their turn to be led into the auction arena.

I was about ready to call it quits, when the pace of the auctioneer picked-up significantly. I suspected he was noticing the shrinking of the crowd and his own fatigue was spurring him to finish the day's business. I gave Nick a nudge with my elbow, signaling that I was ready to leave. About to stand up from the bench where we were sitting, I noticed a pair of horses being led into the ring.

The larger of the two horses appeared to be a young Appaloosa filly and the other was a Haflinger, which is a small draft horse breed. They both looked to be alert and spunky. The Appaloosa was tall and sleek with long legs, a broad chest, and very muscular. This horse was quite a looker, prancing about with her head high and appearing very confident. The second horse was plainer looking; a stocky palomino with a stubby straw-colored tail and mane and seemed to be a companion to the Appaloosa.

I immediately knew I wanted this Appaloosa

filly. I began bidding against two other interested parties. When my bid reached $450.00, my opponents both dropped out. I had bought this horse! Now the auctioneer was pressuring me to buy the other horse. Nick abruptly offered $250.00 for the companion horse and the auctioneer bellowed, "Sold!"

Nick and I were both elated! We hurried to the office to pay and were given our bills of sale. I was handed an envelope containing additional papers with the notation on the front "The Appaloosa, Misty Bright." These were her pedigree papers which denoted her sire and dam; both of which were registered Appaloosas.

We rushed to the holding pen to meet our horses. They stayed close to each other and seemed to be jumpy. The stockman told us they had been placed in the same pen early that morning. They had passed away the long hot auction day by sniffing and licking each other; getting acquainted I suppose.

As we continued observing our horses, a woman approached me asking if we were now owners' of the Appaloosa horse known as Misty. I confirmed her suspicion and following some brief pleasant conversation, she offered to buy Misty at double what I had paid for her. I declined her offer and she departed.

Thirty minutes passed and our horse trailer arrived following my call to a neighbor. The horses loaded easily and we were soon headed home.

As we arrived at the farm dusk was upon us and the horses seemed eager to check out their new home. As we lowered the trailer gate door, they charged out into the barnyard and commenced galloping around as if to communicate their approval of these new accommodations. Suddenly they both took off for the front pasture as if racing. Five minutes later they returned sprinting back to the barn where we were preparing a water trough and a generous portion of sweet horse mix feed for each. They were now safely in a stall and I made my way toward the house, exhausted but eager to announce the news of the two new additions to the family.

Spring in Kentucky, is for many the best season of the year. As the weather warms and Old Man Winter retreats; nature bursts to life flooding one's senses with the sounds, colors, and delightful fragrances of the grasses, blooming trees, and flowers. This April morning began especially early for me. The sun was just beginning to fade the night sky as I headed out to issue a morning greeting to our two new barn boarders. As I neared the barn, I could see the horses were already up and out in their new pasture grazing on the fresh, tender spring grass.

At the horse barn I had erected an antique dinner bell and rang it with a purpose for the first time. Both horses looked-up from their grazing toward the sound of the bell and slowly began making their way toward me. I was a bit surprised by this response and recalled how lively they were last evening.

As they came closer I could see that Misty seemed to be limping, favoring her right front leg. When they entered the barn yard, I stroked their heads and neck then offered each another portion of sweet mix. Horses have a bit of a sweet tooth and this multigrain feed mix is coated lightly with molasses. They took right to it, finishing the treat rather quickly.

As Misty focused on her breakfast, I moved to her side to get a look at that front leg. To my dismay I saw a crusted small scab with a portion being a pink fleshy wound approximately three inches long at the front knee joint. The area appeared to be swollen when compared to the other knee.

During all the excitement yesterday I did not notice anything unusual about her. I deliberated that perhaps she had injured the knee during the transport last night, but now in the morning light I could not detect any fresh bleeding. I immediately called the local Veterinarian stating my concern and he was at the farm within the hour.

A young Vet who had established a practice in our small community, he was well respected and very much liked by the locals. I told him of attending the auction yesterday and only noticing this slight limp this morning. He had a way with large animals as Misty warmed to his stroking her mane and talking to her.

I removed Cole, the Haflinger, from the area and took him to a stall as the Vet continued his examination of Misty's leg injury. Cole watched us intently and did not seem to be content with this short distance separation from Misty.

Following a fifteen minute examination the Vet led Misty to a stall in the barn. He had a concerned look on his face as he confirmed she did indeed have a cut on the right leg and the location of the wound was cause for much concern. He explained to me that a wound on the knee joint would be in an almost constant state of motion, thus impeding the opened area from properly closing and healing. He further cautioned that this type of wound has a low success rate for a full recovery, oftentimes creating a permanent handicap which would require the horse be put down. Treatments for this type injury can be very painful for the animal, expensive for the owner, and rehabilitation most always fails; thus leaving only one humane solution.

The Vet had more bad news. There was evidence on the wound of brown shoe polish which had been applied to temporarily mask the cut just long enough to get the horse sold with an appearance of health. He explained this form of deception is a common place practice or a standard trick of the trade, often used by a seller wishing to take advantage of the prospective naïve buyer. He suggested that I take the horse back to the livestock market and expose the trickery. I might prevail in getting some of my purchase price back, but I knew this would certainly clear the way for Misty to become the acquisition of the X buyer.

The Vet told me Cole was too thin. He did look to be much thinner than he appeared to be yesterday. Here comes another form of marketing trickery. He said many young horses being introduced to the process of breaking them for riding have a hard time adjusting to blankets, saddles, mouth bits, etc. In anticipation of being saddled they will deep breathe, puffing their body up just prior to being tacked-up. Once the gear is tightened on their bulk they will expel the excess air, making a looser more comfortable fit. At the auction just prior to their sale, a blanket or a mouth bit will be applied which triggers this puffing-up reaction by the horse in anticipation of being saddled. This trick temporarily masks their under-weight condition.

All this information was a hard pill to swallow, as I had to acknowledge I had been duped. I asked the Vet if there was a possibility of recovery for Misty. His prognosis was bleak, but we could give it a try. She would have to be placed in a stall and taken out regularly each day for exercise. The wound would be treated with an antibiotic salve. Her diet would need to consist of high protein supplements, fresh hay, and plenty of water. The stall would need to be kept very clean in order to reduce the chance of infection. I would need to be willing to devote four hours each day in this undertaking.

He explained that the leg needed to be walked but for short time periods. Too much exercise would cause what he referred to as "proud flesh." This is an accelerated rate of growth of fleshy tissue which creates "growths" around the wound site, ultimately causing increased lameness and atrophy in the leg joint. He speculated that following a couple of weeks of treatment, he could better establish a prognosis.

I committed to follow the Vet's treatment plan for Misty's injury and to do everything possible to get Cole to a desirable weight. Cole sensed something was up and did not leave Misty's side. His stall was adjacent to her stall so they were separated by just a foot or so. This would be the regime for the next several weeks.

I gathered all the supplies stipulated by the Vet and diligently initiated the treatment program. Every morning Cole was taken out of the barn to pasture and Misty was led into the open barnyard, allowing her to walk around while her stall was being cleaned. I could see she wanted to join Cole out in the expansive pasture, but that would be too taxing on her bad leg.

Later in the morning the wound would have to be cleaned and the medicated ointment reapplied. This was the most challenging aspect of her care. Misty was very temperamental and often fractious. Touching the wound site would set her off. This treatment had to be done in the 12′ x 12′ stall which put me at risk of being kicked or butted off my feet. Brushing her did help to calm her and rubbing her nose gently seemed to almost sedate her into a semi-sleep state. Then I had to move quickly in order to complete the necessary wound care.

Within a few days, she became familiar with the routine and even looked forward to a brushing and nose rub. Her appetite remained good and the wound seemed to look better. Her walking gait also showed improvement, but I knew she still had a long way to go to complete recovery.

Following a full week of treatment, the Vet came by to assess her progress. He prodded and probed the healing wound offering no verbal clue to divulge his findings. Finally finishing the examination he said he was pleased to see evidence of slow healing, no signs of infection or developing proud flesh! Careful not to give me any false hope, he encouraged me to continue with the exact treatment schedule I had in place.

Every afternoon I would return Cole from the pasture to his stall. I was amused observing Misty greeting him and Cole acknowledging her in return. It was obvious that they relished each other's company. Things seemed to be looking up, in spite of a nagging sense of insecurity that I still really did not know what I was doing; executing care interventions in a hit and miss way. I was convinced the clean stall, nourishing special dietary supplements, and the companionship with Cole was the necessary keys to her recovery.

After a month of confinement in the barn, I decided to introduce a change to her course of treatment. It was time to let Misty join Cole in the pasture for a portion of the day. This change was implemented slowly, beginning with only a couple of hours each morning and gradually increasing her pasture time.

The first day I turned her loose to join Cole she began the day pacing around in the enclosed barnyard as usual. Cole was already out doing his morning grazing. Misty was watching me as I walked over to the gate, slowly opening it.

Her eyes widened and her ears perked up when I called her to come to me. In a flash she bolted past me at full stride into the adjoining field, kicking up her hind legs as she ran. Her freedom was immediately noted by Cole and he in turn raced to meet her. They sort of pranced around each other in salutation before racing out to the open pasture.

Observing the two horses having so much "horse fun" brought joy to my heart. I sensed Misty was going to be okay. She was running with no limp, out- pacing Cole, and looking like a racehorse as her long legs fashioned an effortless running gait. I checked on them later and rang the dinner bell which they had come to associate with feeding time. They charged back to the barn seeming to appreciate that there would be generous portions of sweet mix waiting.

This first day of freedom went exceedingly well. By the end of the week she appeared to be fully recuperated, but I wanted the Vet to examine her and confirm this deduction. During this examination of her leg, he did not disguise his pleasure with the findings. Confirming that healthy new tissue had completely sealed the wound with no evidence of proud flesh or abnormal skin growth, and observing her walking gait to be smooth with no favoring to the injured leg, he declared she was ready for all normal activity. In doing so, he opened the gate exposing the pasture where Cole awaited and Misty bounded past him in full stride. Smiling, he offered one last obvious professional opinion, "That horse loves to run!"

After he left, taking his considerable healing skills to what I presumed to be another animal in distress, I relived in my mind many of the past days spent in helping Misty rebound to her present state of vigor. The month had been quite a roller coaster ride for the entire family. A lot of patience was needed and occasionally futile efforts were employed, in our endeavor to instill in this animal a degree of trust that we were doing only those things necessary to make her well, so she could run again without pain. I was content with the realization that we had helped Misty beat the odds and she could now enjoy her new home along with her sidekick, Cole.

Some three months had pasted; both horses were thriving, gaining weight and shedding that look of having been neglected. Regular grooming and a nutritional horse diet made their coats shine as well as sparking growth in their mane and tails. Both became immediate hits with the guests staying at our Bed and Breakfast. They loved the extra attention they were given by the guests which always included softly spoken words of admiration along with friendly hands petting and caressing them. More often than not, this extra attention included a few carrots or apple slices as a treat.

Misty demanded the lion's share of the spotlight always; as Cole seemed unoffended in accepting his subservient role. Their bonding rules had been established by the pair very early on; Misty was the Boss and Cole was the Protector. Cole would soon come of age as a stallion and would have to undergo surgical castration, so he would be making a visit to our Veterinarian friend's office in the near future. Gelding a stallion diminishes their natural aggressive tendencies and enables them to be handled much easier by inexperienced owners, such as me.

The next undertaking would be breaking and training them for riding. Misty would become the first pupil and Cole would follow later. I realized I would need to find an experienced horse handler to take charge. I did not know that there were different schools of thought as to how best to break a horse. I was actually offended by the term "breaking a horse."

This concept in my way of thinking literally means robbing the animal of their singular free-spirit which is God instilled through the infliction of pain; oftentimes at tortuous levels, and in doing so implanting a permanent element of fear in their consciousness if they fail to bend to the commands of the trainer.

The Amish are recognized for their allegedly efficient tactics in breaking a horse for saddle or yoke. It appears that they break the spirit first, draining all the personality from the animal leaving only a robotic creature which will exist solely to function as a mere farming implement. I made some inquiries within the community of my hope of employing an individual with a recognized skill set for training a horse to saddle for pleasure riding.

The first prospective trainer showed up one morning, claiming to be highly experienced with training horses and knowledgeable of all the methods which were used, he wanted to meet Misty. To the barn we went.

He introduced himself by stroking the side of her neck while speaking softly to her. He proceeded to rub and brush her body with a horse comb, relaxing her to the point of her eyelids becoming heavy as if she were about to fall into a sleep. I was familiar with this technique and admired how quickly he seemed to be charming Misty. In a few minutes he proceeded to gently place a rope around her long neck, guiding her from the barnyard into the front pasture. He suddenly yelled at the top of his lungs and Misty immediately pulled her ears back flat as a sign of anger, as her eyes bulged open with fright. I shouted at him, "What are you doing?!!"

He explained to me that this practice was used to get the horse accustomed to loud sudden noises so they would not react by bolting or throwing off their rider. He then began forcefully jerking on her lead rope which caused it to tighten around her neck in an attempt to force her to follow him. "You have to train them to know who's the boss!", he shouted. Misty was becoming highly agitated and trying to run away from this guy. I had seen just about enough of this when he motioned for me to come and take the lead rope. Without thinking I did what he told me.

Misty seemed to calm down a bit sensing I held the rope. She knew me by sight. I was after all, the one who attended to her needs, gave her that sweet mix she was so fond of , and always had a special treat tucked away in my pants pocket for her and Cole. The trainer once again began clapping his hands loudly while whooping and hollering, startling her out of the brief sense of security. She wheeled around and at full gallop took off with me still holding on the rope which was looped around my hand. This all happened so suddenly; I was dragged by her across the pasture for what was a mere few seconds, but the experience of this belly blistering full speed ahead pull remains burned into my memory.

Well, that was the last straw! Thanking him for his demonstration, I sent him on his way. I wondered if he had realized that it was very unlikely I would be interested in contracting for his services. I strongly suspected that he knew exactly how Misty would react, when he enticed me to take hold of the lead rope.

I headed to Barnes &Noble and bought a book about horse training which was authored by a well-known "Horse-Whisperer." The methods of training outlined by this expert were aligned with those of the Native American Indians; ancient approaches which stressed gentler interventions designed to bend, not break the horse's spirit. This was the method I leaned toward, so I committed to give what I had learned reading this book, an amateurs' try.

The next morning I headed to the barn with a heart filled with optimism. I used the brush and comb to curry her muscular body which she always seemed to enjoy and then without much fan-fare I placed the lead rope over her head and then around her neck. This practice was similar to training a dog to walk on a leash. The main difference being this was no 40 pound dog, but an 800 pound horse.

I began our first lesson, promptly realizing I had a big problem. She refused to move. No matter how I tried to persuade, coax, bribe, and beg, she just stared at me and would not budge. Now it was obvious we had an epic battle of wills brewing, and due to her size I would be on the losing end. Misty was not intimidated by me in the least bit; she was quite relaxed as she boldly began to stare me down. I sensed she may in fact be amused with our cat and mouse game, knowing she was getting the best of me.

It was curious to me that she refused to respond to my commands with the lead on, but as soon as it was removed, she followed me and was generally cooperative. Persisting in my effort to get her under my spell, one day I spent an hour coaxing her to follow me with the lead, again with no success. Completely frustrated and swearing under my breath, I removed the rope lead and abruptly turned to walk away. Without warning, she followed and nudged me in the back with her nose. I was so pleasantly surprised by this playful act, I turned to face her and as I was belly laughing, rubbed her nose with a feeling of much affection in my heart.

At that moment Misty and I came to an understanding that would work for both of us. I would no longer attempt to break her will and in turn, she would bend a little more to my requests. I guess one would call this a Mexican stand-off of sorts.

I did not even give serious consideration now, to enlisting Cole as a student in my training effort. He was still a young stallion and I had learned enough to bypass even lesson one with him.

The months passed and they had been

members of our farm family for more than a year. We had established a routine both respected and I watched as they matured into handsome and very sociable horses, enjoyed by everyone they came into contact with. Both horses had become mischievous with some of their encounters with visitors. Misty took to scouting for a pack of cigarettes in the shirt pocket of some of the Bed and Breakfast guests. As they were petting her head and talking to her, she would nuzzle the cigarettes from the unsuspecting individual's pocket, chew the tobacco and spit out the filters. Once I was talking with a fellow who had his back to the barnyard fence. Misty spied a pack of cigarettes in his pocket and leaning her head over the fence and his left shoulder, secured the pack between her lips with the skill of any big city pickpocket. Misty was no respecter of age, or gender. She would steal candy from innocent young children, given the chance.

Cole loved to grab hats off people's heads and run off with them. I was a victim to his shenanigans on several occasions when he would swipe off my head the Amish style straw hats I liked to wear during the hot Kentucky summer days. He was particularly fond of my straw hats, oftentimes eating them as a treat.

Swiping baseball caps was just a fun thing to do, and the caps' protruding bill was simply an irresistible temptation for Cole, who was always looking for something mischievous to do.

I had grown quite content in the company of these two horses and began to consider a quiet, peaceful semi-retirement for the three of us. Think again!

One nice early summer day, the telephone rang and the caller identified himself as Billy Silver- Eagle. He operated a horseback riding stable some twenty miles from the farm. He explained that the proceeding night the barn he was renting which housed his horses had caught fire and was totally destroyed. He needed to find a location where he could temporarily move his horses that had some grassland and water. Having read an article in the newspaper about my Bed and Breakfast, he asked if I would consider boarding his horses for a couple of weeks. He was in a desperate situation with his horses now homeless, he needed help.

I had a ten acre pasture in the back section of the farm which required cutting every couple of weeks. Basically this was a good stand of grass and clover going to waste, so I invited him over to my place to discuss this option further. No sooner had the invitation been extended; he was standing on the front porch knocking on the door announcing his arrival.

With just one look I knew he was to be somewhat of a character. He claimed to be a full-blooded Indian. His chosen attire was a half Indian ensemble with a feathery cowboy flair. He started telling his story almost the minute he arrived. It seemed bad luck had been his constant companion, as he described a string of ill-fated business dealings, bad marriages, and an assortment of health problems which had plagued him for decades.

His latest business endeavor gone badly involved his horseback riding venture. He had acquired ten horses; all of which were older animals and they had all been on the horse-riding circuit for many years. A sudden late night fire burned up the barn and Billy's riding set-up, leaving him and his unfortunate horses out of business. He lived with a girlfriend in a trailer nearby, but now his horses were left with no home or feed lot. I could see how much he cared for his animals as he pleaded his case for a temporary refuge for them as he figured out what to do next.

With only a twinge of reserve, I agreed to board his horses in the short term, until he had time to secure permanent provisions for them after he had decided what he was going to do. He left to make the arrangements necessary to transport his herd later in the day.

I informed the family, of Billy Silver-Eagle's dilemma and the role "we" had accepted in helping him get his life back in order. Each one looked at me as if I had completely lost my marbles. I tried to vindicate my decision by assuring them that Billy's horses would all be maintained in the back pasture away from Misty and Cole. This would cost us nothing, and could even work out to be cost saving as the pasture certainly would not need to be mowed off as long as horses were keeping it grazed down. I even played on their emotions, insuring them what a good plan this was to help a fellow human being as well as these poor homeless animals. Yes, I agreed that Billy Silver-Eagle was a bit idiosyncratic, but I restrained myself from judging him too quickly. Come on now I reasoned, this was a first impression formulated in little over an hour, and after all, we all had our own quirks, right?

The back field where Billy would board his horses had a thick stand of grass and clover which I had sowed a couple of years ago, and fenced it with wire and T- posts, rather than the fancy white wood plank fencing which enclosed the front pastures. Later that evening, Billy arrived with his horse trailers and the horses were quickly unloaded. My first thought when surveying this group was "what a rag-tag bunch of horse flesh!"

They were a hodgepodge of various breeds and half-breeds, all of which seemed to be lethargic and completely detached from their surroundings. They were thin and their coats were dull, unlike my horses that had smooth shiny coats and well-muscled bodies. They apparently existed in a communal existence of misery.

Most likely many years ago they had been broke harshly to saddle and based upon their physical appearance had been provided only minimal sustenance and care, while being worked hard. As I surveyed each one, I could literally count their ribs, which indicated to me that they were malnourished. Voicing this concern to Billy, he shrugged it off while pointing out that they were "work horses, a little on the lean side."

The couple of weeks respite for these horses which Billy had sought after his rented barn had burned to the ground had escalated into weeks and weeks. I thought I was seeing evidence of some improvement in the overall condition of the horses, yet none was gaining the weight needed to look even half-way fit. Billy came to me requesting my approval for him to bring his horse tack trailer to the farm which would enable him to temporarily operate his horse riding operation for "some of his regular customers." He theorized that the ten acre back section would allow for a thirty minute ride and he could use the ticket money for horse feed. If I was in agreement, this would only be for the final month remaining in fall, at which time he would relocate his horses to northern Florida where he planned to open a horse riding business in the milder winter climate.

With some frustration, I agreed to yet another of Billy's supposedly well thought out schemes. Over the next few weeks, only a few stragglers showed up for riding, but the conditions for the horses persisted in growing worse. Winter was to soon be upon us and these horses would require shelter. Billy's bad luck or bad choices continued. I began to suspect he had a developing drinking problem. There were also some disturbing patterns of mistreatment and neglect with the animals which I would not turn a blind cyc to.

In moving Billy's horse riding operation to the farm, he had significantly curtailed the amount of time during the day in which the horses could graze and water. He was now keeping them hitched at his tack trailer most of the time in anticipation of someone showing up wanting to ride. This practice insured that the horses would fail to thrive as their day was spent hitched, unable to exercise or access food and water.

I witnessed an incident in which he had become frustrated with one of the horses and commenced whipping her with a stick. I ran over to him, grabbing the crude whip from his hand, while sternly warning him never to abuse any of these horses again on my property! He stormed off in order to cool off. I took charge of the horse, releasing her to rejoin her friends grazing in the pasture.

Billy liked to use a whip. Billy's personal horse was a magnificent, high- spirited, solid-white Arabian. She was by far the best and youngest horse he owned, yet one day I caught him in the barn where he had put her into a stall and was whipping her relentlessly in quarters too tight for escape. I did not care what this horse had done which provoked Billy's wrath; I stopped this beating immediately and issued my final warning to him about abusing animals on my property.

In addition to my suspicion about Billy's

excessive intake of liquid spirits, I believed he had cut back on the portion of grain he should be feeding his horses. This situation was intensifying toward disaster and I was very concerned.

There were a total of twelve horses on the farm; two of them belonging to me and the remaining ten belonged to Billy. They continued to be separated; Misty and Cole had the barn and front division of property and Billy's horses remained in the ten acre back section, with a fence separating them.

One day I notice that one of Billy's horses had made her way to the backside of the barn where the fence divided the two grazing sections. She was a large older palomino draft horse who was very gentle and laid back. She was just standing there in the same spot. For the next few days, this same horse would reappear about the same time in the day to the same location, where she would stay for about an hour just staring toward the barn as if in somewhat of a daze. She always came alone.

Her behavior perked my interest and it finally dawned on me that her time of arrival each day corresponded to the time I fed Misty and Cole the sweet mix. She was named Buttercup, which suited her well because of her pale yellow color and her sweet nature. As my two horses chowed down on grain feed or sweet mix, she would study them intently, before slowly turning to return to the other horses when they had finished eating. I realized she was hungry, hoping she too would be fed a bit of the sweet mix.

My initial reaction was, whoa; there's no way I am going to start feeding Billy's horses! Yet, Buttercup's persistence pulled at my heart-strings. I eventually gave in and included her each day with a good portion of feed, the same grain or sweet mix given to Misty and Cole. I could actually detect the gratitude she communicated to me in her eyes. Her secret was soon circulated among her horse friends, as each day other horses would be waiting at the backside of the barn along with her; right at feeding time. It was not long before I was feeding all of them.

I confronted Billy with the feeding arrangement which had developed. He confessed that he had no money to buy feed for them; and oh, by the way, his plans to move the herd to Florida at the end of the month had fallen through and he had not found another home for his horses. As he explained yet another sad story to me, I could easily detect the smell of liquor on his breath. So

I am thinking, "You can come up with the money to buy booze, but can't come up with any money to feed your horses!"

What a mess I had gotten into with my willingness to deal with Billy. I now had ten destitute, broken-down, homeless horses, along with a drunken Indian, and the onslaught of winter just around the corner. I had no choice but to continue caring for these horses, as I knew the pasture grass had thinned and about stopped growing. I could not bear having them on my farm knowing they were starving without my advocacy. As expected, my feed bill sky-rocked. It even had gotten to the point where some of the Bed and Breakfast guests became aware of my plight, and I suppose out of a feeling of pity for me and the horses, would make a small charitable donation to the cause, which did help out some.

Things actually came to a head when I called Billy and set a meeting time for us on the following day. He arrived a bit late and before I could utter a word, offered to sell me his entire herd for a rock-bottom price. He was desperate for money and had no choice but to sell his horses.

I could hardly contain myself before bellowing, "No way!" What was I going to do with all these horses and how in the world would I care for them on a long term basis? There were all kinds of obstacles which would make this option impossible; first and foremost I had no barn large enough to shelter all of them for the rapidly approaching winter months ahead. The meeting had been a bust. Billy left. I cannot recall if we made any kind of preliminary plan to address Billy's catastrophe at the time or not; Billy just was gone.

That afternoon Buttercup showed up, along with the others at chow time. As I fed them I realized that I become attached to them and could not be indifferent to their plight. These horses were not as fortunate as mine, who in spite of any earlier distress they may have faced early on in their existence, now enjoyed a stress-free, easy, predictable life. It was so very obvious that Billy's group of horses had lived a hard life; growing old now accustomed to routine neglect, abuse, and mistreatment. It was heart wrenching to consider. Now they were here with me and in my care; like it or not, the reality staring me in the face was that they were totally dependent on me.

That night Billy called me from the hospital explaining that he had been admitted for treatment of an acute attack of kidney stone problems, which apparently was going to leave him out of commission for the foreseeable future. He was refining his earlier offer to sell me all of his horses, due in part to the desperate circumstances he was now faced with. He proposed selling me his "top four" horses for a fair price and throwing in the others, who were older for nothing. Turning up the sales pressure in an obvious effort to play on my sensitivities, he said his only other option was to sell them all at a special price to "guess who."He was pretty sure the glue factory buyer could take them off my hands within a couple of days. His pressure tactic was working. I heard myself telling Billy, "I'll think it over and get back to you in the morning."

I presented the details of this dilemma to the family, who were quick to point out all the obvious reasons that it would be best if we just left it to Billy to make "whatever arrangement" he had to, in order to free himself of the responsibility of these horses. Their final contribution to this family conference was, "Of course, it's your decision." More pressure!

I had trouble getting to sleep that night as I struggled with coming to a decision. I contemplated one alternative and then another. I kept thinking about Buttercup, that big Belgian draft horse who was so well-mannered, sort of a gentle giant, now old and tired and near her end. A horse that had likely spent her life being used and misused by man, while revealing an attitude of forgiveness as evidenced by her gentle, meek behavior.

Lakota was another one of the horses I had become particularly fond of; probably because I knew the particulars of her earlier life. Like my Misty, Lakota was an Appaloosa. She had once been an accomplished barrel racing horse in the western rodeo circuit. She brought a hefty price of $12,000.00 for a past owner who bought, sold, and traded in the western horse markets. She was forced from a highlife in the spotlight of the rodeo as the result of a freak accident which blinded her left eye. This permanent injury abruptly ended her career in the arena. No longer the rodeo star, Lakota was reduced to providing brief pleasure horse rides for those willing to pay the ticket price to her various string of owners'.

When I awoke the next morning, I had reached a decision. Despite all logic, I would buy them, provide them a home, build onto the barn which would afford them shelter, and put them up for adoption. I would become a horse rescuer with a mission, despite lacking funds and much expertise with horses. It gave me a good feeling, knowing I would give them a well-deserved retirement and they would live out their remaining days; no longer underfed and overworked.

With the barn expansion, I included an over-sized stall constructed especially for Buttercup. It was amazing that the horses each knew their assigned stall after the first introduction. Buttercup loved her private quarters, and I would find her there for long intervals during the day as the others had taken to the pasture to graze.

It all worked out well. The horses became adopted members of our family and were really a joy to all of us. One summer, my younger brother and his family came to visit. They were city dwellers from south Florida and farm life was totally foreign to my young niece and nephews. They immediately became enthralled with the free-range chickens and geese, as well as the pair of cows we had. One evening Nick saddled Buttercup and Lakota, the two most trusted to safely let an inexperienced youngster ride on their back, so the kids could have some fun. Nick led them one behind the other around an imagined rink in the front field. Nothing ever went unnoticed by Misty. She watched the goings-on for a bit and then fell in at the rear of the parade, as if beckoning, "ME TOO! ME TOO!"

I had not proceeded with any further attempts to break Misty to a saddle since she had given me that "dragged by the lead rope" ride on my belly. Nick and I got our heads together and plotted an experiment. We saddled Misty, mouth bit and all, and believe it or not; she allowed Nick to mount the saddle as they joined the processional which I was now leading. Don't tell me horses are dumb! My Misty is as smart as they come! She wasn't willing to share center-stage with these two new comers' even if it meant giving in to the saddle.

The years passed by and it's coming upon twenty years since my horse story commenced. I had been successful in placing a couple of the adopted horses in what I knew were good homes for them within our community. The others' lived out their remaining years here at the farm. I would like to think they all finally got a well-deserved respite from their earlier sad existence. Maybe like a little piece of horse Heaven here on Earth.

Eventually time took its toll and they left me, one-by-one. I grew to anticipate what was to come. In every instance, the horse some three days before the end would refuse to eat the grain or sweet mix, no matter how much they were coaxed to do so. On the fourth day, I would find their lifeless carcass lying in the section of pasture where they had chosen to graze each and every day. This sequence of happenings led me to find old Buttercup one early morning, right in the pasture spot she claimed as hers.

Now it's just Misty, Cole and me, back to where the journey began. They remain inseparable and continue to delight in entertaining the guests who vacation at the farm. Now in the prime of their lives, they continue to race each other from time to time early on crisp mornings. Misty always wins, but Cole doesn't ever seem to mind.

I appreciate the joy all of these horses have brought into my life, the lives of my family, and the lives of the many children who have accompanied their parents or grandparents to stay awhile at our little farm. Yes, most particularly the kids, who delight in feeding them apple slices and carrots. We have hosted families from all across the United States and many who have traveled from foreign countries; most of them drawn to the area to explore and vacation at Mammoth Cave National Park. These guests have all been introduced to our rescue horses.

In a sense they pulled their own weight, so to speak, by attracting many guests to our Bed and Breakfast who had a sole interest in visiting rescue horses. Their special designation as being a rescue horse made them all the more intriguing; perhaps because their storied past was sad and disturbing, yet with their own eyes our guests could see the happy ending.

Years ago it dawned upon me, that during their well-deserved retirement, they sort of took on the role of ambassadors for the forgotten, abused, and neglected horses that are sometimes hidden away, expecting to be discarded, awaiting their fate with the X buyer. They were not even aware of how their plight may weigh on someone's conscience and heart. Perhaps someone who would in turn; at some time have an opportunity to speak out in support of horse rescuing, pass along these horse rescuing values to a child, or even rescue a horse themselves.

During my adulthood, I have been presented with a number of unexpected dilemmas or circumstances. I have come to understand that these situations are often times of God. I think He keeps track of the decisions you make and how you handle these opportunities. I believe that, because it was never even in my mind to become a horse rescuer, not in my wildest dreams. In fact, at the time, I saw the whole escapade with Indian Billy and his horse riding operation, as a big pain in the rear-end, in fact a mess I had gotten in because of dealing with him in the first place. In the final analysis, I was being offered a commission from Heaven above; all I had to do was choose to accept the challenge.

The way was made crystal clear for me during those sleepless hours I spent pondering the fate of ten haggard and homeless horses. Sometimes I wonder if it was I who rescued them; or if in reality, they were sent to rescue me.

On the farm

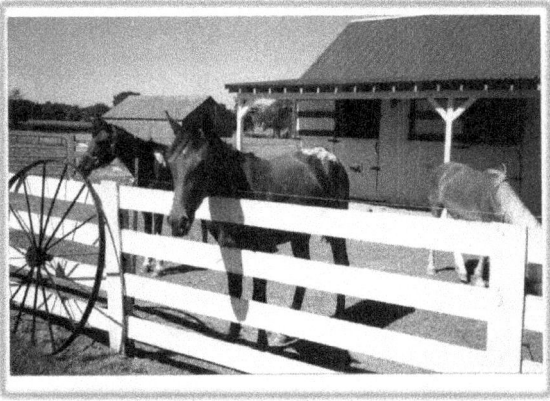

Left to right: Lakota, Misty, and Cole.
Misty and Cole had been on the farm for a couple of years.

Dylan, Hannah, and Cole

Dylan and Misty

Hannah and Misty

Bill grooming Lakota

Chapter VII

Manifest Destiny

Golden Silence Returns

Today the cavern is in harmony with the rhythm of nature; the ebbs and flows of which are best captured at the cave's foyer where the light is diminished into the darkness. It is only here, unique to caverns with the vestibule at a southern exposure; which the morning sunlight is permitted to peek in, then to be slowly pulled back as the earth moves along its natural orbital path; providing a visual measurement of each season's passage of time. Yet, it is within the consuming blackness, the mystique of an underground world shelters all its mysteries and secrets. Many inquisitive cave explorers, in time will consent that some things are left better to wonder about; as the ancient cavern gently casts its spell.

It is true, that silence is golden for alas, finally a welcomed quietness would flood all the chambers and passages, settling in the most exalted sanctuary. Wondrous tranquil peace within the quiet solitude, allowed the cavern to rest and breathe once again, as only soft natural cave sounds could be heard reverberating in the darkness.

In time, the once hallowed ground violated for decades would begin to heal its wounds, through purging and cleaning the impurities acquired through the errant conduct of contemporary humans. Since the erecting of the great iron sentinel, only persons with a reverence of its opulence and a conviction for its protection, are allowed to cross the threshold and delight in the treasures within.

One cannot deny the Creator's handiwork in the majestic sculptured natural beauty of the cavern; or refute His omnipresence within, giving one a sense that this primordial site has the aura of a living, vibrant entity. There is a cave legacy which oddly parallels its earliest human inhabitant; essentially a joint fate, closely intertwined and seemingly a near mirror reflection of each other; separate, but commonly sharing the same passage of time and space.

A local hobbyist spelunker from an adjoining county, after spending time exploring the passageways within this cave, was inspired to compose the following poem:

Secrets

Who was the first; Oh, silent cavern, to walk your ancient halls?
Who first smelled your dampened earth; and touched your scalloped walls?
Your ceiling hanging like a garden grand; with domes that reach so high.
Did he stand and gazed in wonder, at sights so pleasing to the eye? Did he see your mighty canyons; with torches made of cane?
And did he sit beside your sparkling lake, Warmed by the flames?
Keep secret your mysteries,
And swear you'll never tell.
Some things are best to wonder about; as you gently cast your spell.

Terry Davis Scottsville, KY

Within these cavern walls, those ancient dwellers had an appreciative understanding of nature; they experienced the impact of the changing seasons and valued the bounties from the earth which sustained their life.

Man could perceive a Designer; one who

interacted with them in a direct and intimate way each day, through the physical world. The Great Benefactor was worthy of praise, veneration, and worship.

Over generations, the advancement of Deity sanctification increased, and the cavern became a Holy Sanctuary; where the mortal and Divine communed in fellowship. Thus, a spiritual awakening ignited a light within the human heart; changing everything as the spirit would seek to become the master over the carnal.

Be Ye Holy, For I Am Holy
Leviticus 11: 44-45

In the final analysis, the cave sanctuary would be where all roads in this mystical journey would begin and end for this nomadic people. This is an exalted place where man encountered the omnipresent Creator, and through faithful worship and praise which acknowledged His holiness; man endeavored to attain God's approval and protection.

For countless generations, the wandering tribes would be drawn back to this sacred place. Reentering the Holy chamber, they reinforced their faith while securing a pathway for all those to come, also seeking a more consecrated life.

From Looting and Desecration to Public Service

God does not change. Today, even in a more modern secular world, the cavern still resonates with His Holy Omnipresence. A new breed of cave explorer, who is a hybrid of scientist and steward, encounter the Creator within the ancient halls of this cave. Although they have a systematic mindset, they appreciate and respect the cavern's heralded Holy past. Most are intrigued by the earliest inhabitants' liaison with the Creator, which continued for hundreds of years within the darkness of this cavern.

Archaeologists who have conducted research in these ancient chambers; speculate about the relationship between primitive man and nature, as drawn in the thin mud veneer on the stone walls For them, God was ever present in nature; a Benefactor who provided for and supplied all human needs for survival and procreation.

The mud glyph testimonials memorialize a people's faith declarations by hallmarking a great spiritual awakening. These visual tributes are akin to voices from antiquity that is frozen in time; imploring those who would pay heeds, to consider their adoration and glorification for the

God of all. The cave, impervious to time, still mysteriously stirs the Spirit that dwells within the human heart.

Hence, the cavern continues to inspire. Since 1995 scientific research is perpetually conducted within the cave, which is formed by soluble limestone rock. Geologists are focused on understanding the hydrogeology and geochemistry of karst water sources. Waterfalls within the cave are used to study and monitor the environmental challenges with flooding; land stability and water supply in this Kentucky cave, which are mimicked in fragile karst geology sites worldwide.

A new era of a manifest destiny is in the making. For more than twenty years, the grotto researchers have collaborated with colleagues in China's vast limestone karst regions, sharing their research results. Consequently, under the umbrella of the United Nations Educational, Scientific, and Cultural Organization (UNESCO), water-related scientific programs benefit mankind with one of God's vital natural resources, life sustaining water. The WKU alumni magazine **Spirit**; SUMMER 2017 issue; pg. 30, "**WKU professor, alumnus, receives China's top science award**; is a recounting of the university's two decade long involvement in

China; bringing fresh ground water sources to millions of rural Chinese, who's quality of life is positively impacted each day, as a result of the on-site research done in this Kentucky cave.

This ancient southern Kentucky cavern continues to reveal secrets hidden within. Puzzles when unraveled confirm to us the benevolence of the Great Benefactor; the omnipresent Spirit so loved and worshiped from antiquity.

Chapter VIII

Epilogue

Reflections

As I reminisce back over the years, I feel blessed and honored to have played a role in the wonderful and exciting events which shaped the dramatic outcomes that have taken place at this Native American Sacred Site Cavern. At my first encounter, I knew this was no ordinary cave. However, being a novice, I viewed it as an earthly orifice, concealed in a black void; harboring mysteries of the unknown. The existence of the cave was only known to some within the rural agricultural area; being an uncharted cavern in the 20th century, and never having been commercialized or opened to the public. Little did I know this grotto was an obscured "diamond in the rough. "

New discovery and enlightenment would almost overnight, transform the once blank, black void of a cave ravaged by looters and vandals, into a world class landmark secured site. However, for me the site's hallmark signature legacy is showcased in man's relationship with the Almighty Creator. This is a distinctive cave, where the mortal found God in the dark; giving birth to a great spiritual awakening, thus leading a nomadic people into the light.

Because of my intimate connection with this cave over the years of discovery and fortification; I was also graciously rewarded with my own mid-life spiritual awakening. I felt God's leading personally and witnessed with wonder as **His** will was being worked through the many human vessels of **His** choosing, to achieve **His** will for **His** cave sanctuary, and for **His** intended purposes for a greater good for all of mankind. I am forever grateful to have been witness to His promise, "And we know that in all things God works for the good of those who love Him, who have been called according to His purpose." (Romans 8:28). **Trust in God.**

The End

Notes:

Additional recommended readings:

When a Mustard Seed Grows, "From an Act of Faith to an Act of Congress," William J. Marohnic, Amazon.com, 2013

The Miracle of the Conscience, "A Portal to the Heavens," William J. Marohnic, Amazon.com, 2015

Author's Bio

Bill Marohnic has been a Kentucky resident for 40 years. He is a graduate of the University of Kentucky. Currently spending his days as a farmer an Innkeeper, and a horse rescuer. Here he is enjoying time on the farm with his two grandchildren, Dylan and Hannah.

www.ingramcontent.com/pod-product-compliance
Lightning Source LLC
Chambersburg PA
CBHW072002040426
42447CB00009B/1448